If one woman told the truth about her life, the world would split open.

Muriel Rukeyser

Permission to Rest

How to
cultivate a
life of self-care,
rejuvenation, and
nurturing the spirit

Debra Mae White

© 2014 by Debra Mae White

All rights reserved. No part of this publication may be reproduced, stored in a retrieval system or transmitted, in any form or by any means—electronic, mechanical, photocopying, recording or otherwise—without prior written permission from the publisher, except for the inclusion of brief quotations in a review.

For information about this title or to order other books and/or electronic media, contact:

All Abundance, Inc.
800 Bering Drive
Suite 227
Houston, TX 77057
Debramaewhite.com
dws@debramaewhite.com

This work is solely for personal growth and education. It should not be treated as a substitute for professional assistance, therapeutic activities such as psychotherapy or counseling, or medical advice. In the event of physical or mental distress, please consult with appropriate health professionals. The application of protocols and information in this book is the choice of each reader, who assumes full responsibility for his or her understandings, interpretations, and results. The author and publisher assume no responsibility for the actions or choices of any reader.

Printed in the United States

Cover and book design by 1106 Design

ISBN 978-0-9904524-0-9 Softcover

ISBN 978-0-9904524-1-6 eBook

To my daughters, Noelle Marie, Aleasha June, and Hollye Michelle, and to all the daughters of the universe who have yet to come.

Contents

PREFACE	Walking the Line	x
INTRODUCTION	Super Woman: The Need for Rest	1
CHAPTER ONE	Adella's Story: Crashing, Burning, and Rising Again	9
CHAPTER TWO	The Seduction of Overwork	21
CHAPTER THREE	Finding Your Barometer: How Imbalance Shows Up in Your Life	27
CHAPTER FOUR	Signs and Stages of the Call to Rest	35
CHAPTER FIVE	Permission Granted	47
CHAPTER SIX	The Science of Rest	55
CHAPTER SEVEN	A Matter of Time	63

CHAPTER EIGHT	The Why	71
CHAPTER NINE	Pushing Through	85
CHAPTER TEN	Giving It Up	93
CHAPTER ELEVEN	Facing Fear	99
CHAPTER TWELVE	Valuing Yourself	103
CHAPTER THIRTEEN	Margo's Story: Healing from the Inside Out	109
CHAPTER FOURTEEN	It's Your Turn Now: Midlife Comes Calling	121
CHAPTER FIFTEEN	Longing	125
CHAPTER SIXTEEN	Prescription for Play	129
CHAPTER SEVENTEEN	Meander	133
CHAPTER EIGHTEEN	Twiddle	139
CHAPTER NINETEEN	Daydream and Stargaze	143
CHAPTER TWENTY	Engage in Frivolity	147
CHAPTER TWENTY-ONE	Watch the Wind	153
CHAPTER TWENTY-TWO	Sit in Silence	157
CHAPTER TWENTY-THREE	Intimacy with the Unknown	161
CHAPTER TWENTY-FOUR	Will the Real Me Please Stand Up?	167
CONCLUSION	Sunset in Sedona	171
ACKNOWLEDGEMENTS		175
RECOMMENDED RESOURCES		181

PREFACE
Walking the Line

For most of my adult life, fear was the big motivator. I thought I would go broke if I didn't work hard, be forceful, and use might to make my reality into what I wanted it to be. Fearful and anxious, I would wake up, dart out of bed, put on a blue suit, and prepare for battle.

In 1975 I entered the high-stakes, high-pressure financial world and in the 1980s began studying to become a Certified Financial Planner (CFP)®. There were quotas to meet and sales contests where I was compared with my colleagues. Management pushed us advisors to perform or be fired. Plus, as a young female in a male-dominated profession, I had to prove that I was better and more competent than my male counterparts. One manager I worked for told me I didn't belong in the financial business and should go home and have a baby. I felt I had to prove him wrong, to prove I had what it took to succeed.

When I did start a family, I had a strong desire to provide a good quality of life for my children. This meant not only providing for them financially, but also finding the time to attend school events and drive to after-school activities. Playing the dual role of mother and professional advisor was a daily stressor.

The only travel I did during the years I was building my financial-planning practice was trips sponsored by the firms I affiliated with. I remember attending one conference that brought in a personal-development speaker as part of the agenda. He looked at the audience and asked, "How many of you think you are on vacation?" I raised my hand. The speaker's eye swept across the room and said, "If you have your hand up, you are a workaholic." That was my first clue that my life was out of balance, and it was a defining moment for me—the awareness moment. I became aware that I was working way too much, and I made my mind up to take a real vacation someday. But I then convinced myself that the vacation could come only when the needs of my business were covered first.

As my practice grew more successful, I felt the pressure to meet and manage the expectations of my clients. My personal desire to help people only added to that pressure. Often I would take on any client who needed help, whether or not they were a good fit for my financial practice and even if they could barely rub two pennies together. Day or night, I'd meet demands for appointments, even if they robbed me of sleep or time to myself.

The day-by-day, simmering stress suddenly rose to a boil when I experienced my own financial crises. My first marriage fell apart, and I became a single mother. Shortly after I met my present husband and remarried, we became embroiled in an intense custody battle with my ex-husband that left us emotionally and financially depleted. We had to sell our home and downsize in order to pay off our debt from the custody suit. In essence, we started our financial lives over from scratch.

All this time, sugar was my primary stress reliever. I always kept candy bars close by when I would work late. I could go for hours on a Butterfinger. Physically, I experienced low-energy periods when the sugar high would wear off, and mentally, I'd have to psych myself up to keep going. Emotionally, I would overreact to a situation or find myself in tears for no specific reason. When I did make small attempts to manage my life, I would inevitably end up feeling guilty. For example, once, when I declined to help a colleague on a committee, she overtly criticized me, and that night I came home and cried myself to sleep, thinking I wasn't good enough because I couldn't pile on yet another commitment.

Periodically I sought help through counseling, but that was an expensive luxury I couldn't always afford. I kept overworking because I believed that so many people were counting on me—my husband, my kids, my clients, and my colleagues. If I stopped to take a breath, I thought their lives would fall apart. My family needed the money to maintain our lifestyle. Even if we had been financially independent, I couldn't face abandoning my clients. I feared letting down those I loved. I thought that if I took care of my own needs, something or someone else would end up neglected and suffer.

I kept up my exhausting pace for three decades because I felt I had no other choice.

In 2005, my thirtieth year in the financial industry, my sisters, my mother, and I made a trip to the Texas hill country retreat known as The Crossings, where poet David Whyte was offering a weekend workshop. Whyte's gifted performance led us all into the stillness within. One day during the retreat, I wandered onto an outcropping of limestone set beside a bed of brilliant bluebonnets. When I closed my eyes to ponder that afternoon's lesson, I heard a voice within say, "You are exhausted and need to rest."

Moreover, the voice continued, "This is your new calling: you are called to write about *rest*, as your next career."

My mind immediately clouded up with fear. How could I shift into a new career, much less a career as a

Preface: Walking the Line

writer? How would I support myself? I would have to sell my house!

"Your home will not be lost, but you will have to give up your current career," the voice said.

"No, no, no, not me," I thought. "I am a financial planner. This is the only thing I am." I couldn't imagine giving up my income or my identity.

Whether the voice was my own spirit speaking or the angels talking to me from heaven above, I will never know. But I was certain that I had been given divine guidance.

Spirit called, but at that moment, I just couldn't bring myself to answer. I came home from the retreat and continued doing what I had been—working too hard, resting too little, fretting too much. I continued to struggle to be all things to all people—a good wife, a caring mother, an attentive advisor, a professional leader, and a supportive colleague. All of these roles overshadowed self-care.

That was until I received three wake-up calls.

One afternoon in 2007, I opened my mailbox and found legal papers. For the first time in thirty-two years of financial practice, I was being sued. The suit was a baffling betrayal. I had done nothing wrong, and the client had lost no money. My insurance carrier called it a nuisance suit and wrote the accuser a $35,000 check. The settlement felt like a knife in my heart. I had had a clean career for decades, and even though I was not at fault, this incident would cloud the rest of my days as a financial professional. Every time I would do business thereafter, I would stumble over this episode.

My emotions got the best of me during this time. I found myself ranting and raving about overregulation of the financial industry and the injustice of the legal system. In my view, clients were being bated into filing lawsuits, and I was a victim. It didn't take much to drive me to tears. Instead of seeing the suit as a sign telling me to slow down, I swallowed the bitter pill and pushed onward. After all, I had a daughter in college to support, a husband who was trying to get his healthcare practice off the ground, and our home to maintain.

The second wake-up call came a year later. My husband and I were ready to return from an anniversary trip in Scotland on September 12, 2008, when we received an email from our airline. It said we could not fly home to Houston because Hurricane Ike was about to make landfall there. When we finally made it home three days later, the Gulf Coast had been badly battered, water was scarce, and our house was without power. That same day, the U.S. stock market reacted to the breaking news of bank failure and began a free fall.

For the first time in my career, I realized how little control I had over my clients' financial outcomes. My days were spent making one phone call after the next to calm

Preface: Walking the Line

investors, but these calls did little to calm my own nerves. My nights were sleepless; my days were spent huddled with my colleagues filled with fear. My blood pressure started to skyrocket. My monthly menstruation turned to torturous and excessive bleeding. With every passing day, I became more emotionally spent.

As the months wore on, none of the tried-and-true remedies of past market declines proved effective. The U.S. government was unable to arrest the stress of the country's financial system, and I was unable to stop the stress of living my life. The more effort I gave my work, the more exhausted I became.

One night I arrived home in tears, and my husband asked me if I had gone hormonal on him. That was my third wake-up call. I realized my life had become unsustainable. It was as if I were sinking underwater and could not hold my breath anymore. I knew I could no longer keep up the pace I'd been running at or the facade of holding it all together when, in fact, I was emotionally crumbling. Suddenly, I couldn't bear to go forward because I thought I was failing to perform the roles I believed were mine to handle.

In December 2008, I checked into a hospital for a hysterectomy. My doctor prescribed what seemed to me to be an absurd amount of time to heal: weeks of bed rest and six months of "taking it easy."

"Rest or relapse. It's your choice," he said.

Physically, mentally, emotionally and spiritually depleted, I surrendered. After three wake-up calls, I finally got the message that at some point I would have to let go of my financial practice. In the meantime, self-preservation required me to find a new path, one that led away from the frantic pace. I started taking a hard look at what I could change in my life to make a difference.

Professionally, I made a commitment to reduce my workdays and hours, and I stopped taking new clients. Then I found a business partner to help me with my workload, and we explored a business transition plan. When our strategy was put in place, I communicated with my existing clients about the changes we were making.

On a personal level, I deepened my spiritual practice and set about learning to write. I began taking writing classes and getting involved in spirit-based writing groups. I started looking within instead of outside myself for life direction. I made the decision to listen to my inner guidance and to go where I was called.

After my recuperation, a meditative technique my husband and I had learned a few years prior became my refuge. The more I committed myself to taking time to practice the meditation, the more peace I experienced.

Lessons from a class I had once taken based on Julia Cameron's book *The Artist's Way* came back to me, reminding me to take walks in nature, take time to experience beautiful art, and write in my journal. During this time, the voice I'd heard in my head that day I sat on a rock in the hill country started speaking again. The messages were clear and consistent: *Rest and write. Get in touch with your needs. Learn how to rest. Make rest a regular life practice. Rest and write about resting.*

For over three decades, I had relied on immense effort, strategy, and swift, decisive action to achieve my success. Today, I am fully entrenched in the new pace of life I had resisted. The practice of resting and receiving guidance has now become a daily regimen for me, and it has given my life a vastly different tone. That tone is based on balancing how much time I work and how much time I rest, how much time I take care of others and how much time I nurture myself.

My self-care includes:

- Setting parameters in my work life, including having clearly defined work days and hours.
- Being kinder and gentler to myself.
- Making time for my spiritual activities.
- Mentally challenging fearful thoughts when they arise.
- Noticing my feelings sooner—before they become too intense for me to contain.
- Listening closely to my body.

My thoughts, feelings, and body are my barometers. By watching them carefully, I can tell when I'm being pulled away from my central core. If I start worrying, I know my thinking has veered off track or that somehow I've bought back into believing my prosperity and wellbeing hinge on outside forces. If I feel sad or angry, I allow myself to explore why I am having those feelings and to work through them. Instead of dismissing my emotions, I look deeper. Is there a message I have not acknowledged? If negative emotions surface, I go back to nurturing myself until I regain my equilibrium and can integrate what life is saying to me.

Giving myself permission to rest is a work-in-progress for me, and these days, my success is measured by how much I walk my talk. My body has ways of telling me when I am crossing the line with too much physical activity, negative thinking, or stuck emotions. When the heels of my feet begin cracking, for instance, I know I must correct my course at once. My feet will literally throb until I put them up and allow myself to rest.

My situation is not unique. Most women face many of the same stressors, pressures, and problems that I have encountered. You probably see some of your own life between the lines on these pages. The good news is that if I figured out how to turn my life around, you can too.

This book will teach you how to finally take seriously the need to rest. You will see that not resting is already costing you dearly and in more ways than you realize. The consequences of not resting are far worse than what will happen if you make the time to rest.

We will go beyond how to rest and dig deep into why you think you can't rest, exposing any guilt and fears to be healed. By giving yourself permission to rest, you will restore your vitality, gain clarity on what you value, and enhance your connection with loved ones. Improved efficiency will lead to increased productivity, and prosperity will follow. You will no longer be blindsided by an emotional rollercoaster or wake up plagued by physical ailments that threaten to topple your life. Regular rest opens the door to your own inner guidance system, which knows exactly when and how to bring life back into balance. You may even begin to notice that, day in and day out, you are happy for no specific reason.

Don't wait until a crisis—a physical, mental, or emotional breakdown—forces you to rest. You have the tools at your fingertips to make small changes now and create a lifelong resting practice. Make a choice in this moment to give yourself the rest you deserve.

INTRODUCTION
Super Woman: The Need for Rest

We hurry through our days numbing ourselves to the deeper flow of our lives. We feel shallow and push ourselves to live harder when what we need is to live more deeply and quietly.

Julia Cameron, *Walking in This World*

"I don't have enough time. I've got so much to get done; there is no time for me."

"Everyone depends on me. I am exhausted. When is it my turn?"

"I've just got to find a minute to spare!"

On the surface, you are keeping it all together. Somehow all the balls are still in the air. Yet you wonder how long you can ignore that empty, aching feeling in your gut. When will the longing for your own self-care consume you?

Or maybe you lament how you used to do more at one time than you can handle now. The pressure of what you expect to accomplish weighs heavily on you. "Why can't I measure up anymore?" you cry to yourself. To add insult to injury, you are fast becoming your own worst critic.

Or perhaps you realize your life is bedlam. You feel underappreciated and at times downright used. You're driven to do it all, and you have no time left to enjoy life. You can afford houses, cars, and clothes, but feel you can't afford to take time to rest. You have heard about living in the moment, but all you can see are moments slipping away. There seems no way to put an end to the madness.

Or perhaps you've hit bottom, and you know it. Your emptiness within is gnawing at you, and your soul is starving for attention. But because you've completely depleted your energetic resources, you don't even know what you really need, much less how to begin giving it to yourself.

Sound familiar?

If this does, you're not alone. I, like so many women, lived through all of these situations, again and again, throughout my adult life.

When the global financial collapse came in 2008, I found myself grasping for something to keep me sane. My stable, lifelong financial advisory career, based on tried and true techniques, quickly transformed into chaos for reasons that were beyond my control. In the months that followed, I realized that as a woman working in a male-dominated industry, I had unconsciously chosen to adopt a cultural drive to achieve as a means of proving my worth. After decades of indoctrination into a results-oriented society, I was unprepared for burnout. Yet in retrospect, burnout was the inevitable consequence of expending an exhaustible energy supply. No one had taught me how to probe the big questions, the deep-seated reasons I was living my life in an unsustainable way.

A catchy jingle from the late 1970s and early 1980s perpetuated the Super Woman myth and epitomized what almost every American girl, including me, thought she wanted to become. The lyrics used in a television commercial for Enjoli perfume, patterned after a song written by Jerry Lieber and Mike Stoller and sung by Peggy Lee in 1963, went something like this:

> I can bring home the bacon
> fry it up in the pan
> and never let you forget you're a man
> 'Cause I'm a woman—spelled W, O, M, A, N

Somewhere along the way, the Super Woman myth gave birth to the idea of multitasking. First the goal was to do it all, and then the goal was to do it all at one time.

Permission to Rest

Constant motion has created a contemporary disease my husband labels "Do I Tis," the drive to keep doing. The message is that you must do something to be someone. Trying too hard to do too much is an impossible task, yet many women will persist and die trying.

Rest is the solution to this modern-day problem. We deserve to take time in our lives to experience life without an agenda, to get in touch with who we truly are and how to meet our inner needs.

Rest is not about getting more sleep. Rest is about rejuvenation. True rest feeds you mentally, emotionally, and spiritually, as well as physically. Rest is a state of being, linking body, emotion, mind, and spirit in a way that renders you an open vessel for receiving nurturance and inspiration. Rest is a vital source of life-giving energy that must become a lifetime priority instead of a luxury. When it does, you will find your productivity during active times increased, your creativity enhanced, and your perspective on life profoundly shifted. In essence, regular rest will lead you to a richer life. Rest can also be a catharsis, the process of letting go of what does not support you and taking in what enlivens you. Rest allows your life to move forward gently, so that you can integrate the wisdom you have garnered and allow the next best version of yourself to emerge.

You don't need to be a professional woman to benefit from rest. Homemakers and those caring for growing families or elderly parents often work harder than those who go to an office. If being a caregiver is your circumstance, perhaps it is even more imperative for you to hear the call. In the words of New Thought performer Karen Drucker, how good is it to give to others when you are cheating yourself?

This book is a map that will take you into the seat of your struggles and help you uncover the messages your soul wants you to hear. *Permission to Rest* provides a soft, subtle process that fosters giving gifts to yourself and gets you to that place where your inner wisdom can emerge, the quiet place inside you where all the answers await.

There are lessons I have discovered as I've learned to live a life in which nature and spirit are balanced with finance and family. There are stories from those who have been in your shoes and lived to tell about it, and there are exercises and ideas that can bring you back home to yourself.

Although the process of the book is gentle and supportive, that doesn't mean it will always be comfortable. The questions this book poses may cause you to confront your fears. What real challenges are you facing? What life conditions have put you into overload? Where do you place the blame for not being able to take time for yourself? They may also reveal some uncomfortable truths and issues smoldering beneath the surface of your choices. For example, you may discover that you were compromising your own needs without realizing it. You may discover a propensity to please others—your spouse, your parents, your kids, your boss. You may find that your image of what a woman should be is based on an unrealistic television commercial rather than your soul. Perhaps you have been caught in the trap of trying to be perfect. Or you may realize that you're using exhaustion as a way of hiding from what doesn't work in your life.

All of these questions lead to what is perhaps the most important question of all: what simple, incremental steps could you take today that will help you lead a healthier, more fulfilling existence?

Keep this book at your bedside, if possible. The ethers around your sleep time will pick up your desires and begin working magic. If you end your day realizing your well has run dry, open to one of the ideas for rest at the end of a chapter and put that practice on the top of your to-do list for tomorrow.

In time, you will experience this paradox: keeping your commitment to your own heart will generate more heart from those around you. As one of my friends said, "I notice that when I am sweeter to myself, my husband and daughter are sweeter to me." Yet the benefits of learning a resting practice go beyond improving your relationships to improving your health, longevity, and spirituality.

The widely read New Thought author Neale Donald Walsch writes of the problems facing humanity and our

Introduction: Super Woman: The Need for Rest

planet. The solution he proposes is also the solution to women's problems of being overburdened and exhausted. He accuses us of attempting to solve the world issues by throwing money or political solutions at them and begs us to answer the question of why we continue this tack when it is clear the root issue is not an economic or political problem. The world has a *spiritual* problem, he points out. Spirit is what is lacking in our lives. A connection to the source of all life has been lost somewhere in our pursuit of material success. It is this very starvation of the spirit that is sabotaging our lives. Walsch suggests our challenges must be addressed at the level of spirit.

As it turns out, stopping to rest is the first step on a greater journey toward solving the real problem. After all, how can any woman address her own fulfillment and spiritual needs when she won't even pause long enough to close her eyes? *Permission to Rest* teaches you how take that first step and make rest a regular practice, so you can begin to address the state of your life from the level of spirit.

Before you begin, let me give you a gift:

You have permission to not be perfect.

My doctor actually wrote these words on his prescription pad and handed it to me one day along with my other prescriptions. The words stunned me, and perhaps they are just as stunning to you. I give you permission to value yourself more than perfection or how well you please others.

Idea for Rest: Conscious Breathing

Take a moment, right now, and close your eyes. Breathe deep, like the Buddha would tell you to do. Repeat this phrase after me: "All I have to do today is breathe out and breathe in." If you learn to listen to your breath, you will soon discern the call to rest, and that is where the healing will begin.

CHAPTER ONE

Adella's Story: Crashing, Burning, and Rising Again

I have arrived. Here and now, I am not running anymore. I have been running all my life, but now I am deciding to stop because I have learned that life is here. When you stop, happiness starts to be possible.

Thich Nhat Hanh, *You Are Here*

Adella wanted rest, but it was something she thought she could afford to do without. She would only allow herself to rest when a flu or illness overtook her. Then, as soon as she felt a slightest bit of improvement, she would jump right back into her life full force.

When I met Adella, she was a vivacious woman married to the man of her dreams. She and her husband,

Don, were connected through their love of performing and had combined their families of teenagers. Don was an engineer by day and a stand-up comic by night. Adella's career leading corporate seminars confirmed that she was a natural in front of an audience. She loved to speak, but she also loved to sing, dance, and act. Adella and Don came together with the common goal of spending their days doing what they loved the most—being on stage. Soon after marrying, they sold their home and purchased their own performance venue.

Adella juggled all the day-to-day business of a theater, which included creating, collaborating, and presenting the shows. She was responsible for scheduling, sales, and minding the books as well. Weekends were spent honing her craft as a performer and appearing on stage. The plan was for Don's income to pay the bills until Adella got the theater up and running. Adella was up to the task, as she had been a wellspring of vitality for most of her life. Yet over time, it became clear that spending her days overdoing even those activities she loved was damaging her health.

In November 2002, Adella noticed that her body was changing. Not yet fifty years old, she wondered why she was constantly ill. As soon as she would get over the flu, she would come down with strep throat. None of her illnesses were life threatening, but all of them were life disrupting. For two and a half years, she battled feelings of utter despair and toughed it out, living for what she could grab from life when she felt functional. But gradually those times became fewer and farther between.

After a battery of medical tests that spanned many months, the doctors scratched their heads and labeled Adella's problem as an autoimmune disease, a modern medical way of acknowledging that, frankly, they had no idea why a seemingly healthy human being comes down with one illness after another. Adella kept promising herself that if she passed through menopause, the tiredness and the weight gain, the stress and the pain, would stop. But time moved on, and these things did not stop.

On August 4, 2005, the crash came. Adella had allowed herself a rare escape, a day at the beach. She had planned to stay the night there and return home the next morning. She had envisioned watching the sunrise with her favorite cup of coffee in hand.

Instead, Adella woke up at 6 a.m. in her seaside hotel room, screaming from pain that ran from head to toe. At first, she could not move her body. Slowly, painstakingly, she began the intense effort of rousing one muscle at a time. Three hours later, she entered her vehicle and drove forty minutes back home, sobbing and feeling searing pain the entire way.

Don immediately rushed her to the emergency room. Once again, the tests revealed nothing, and she was sent home with pain so bad that it spurred an evening of vomiting. Before dawn, she was back to the emergency room. This time Adella was told she had experienced an acute onset of rheumatoid arthritis, and she was given a shot of prednisone. She was not convinced of the diagnosis. A voice inside of her kept saying, "I don't think so. Pumping me with drugs is not the answer."

After the second emergency room visit, she sat in her car in the hospital parking lot, mulling over what the medical staff had told her. She noticed that a moth was trapped inside the car and flapping frantically at the passenger-side window. All that separated the winged creature from freedom was a thin pane of glass. Frustrated, the moth continued to try to break through to the other side. Adella felt the struggle of the tiny insect and pressed the button beside her to trigger the downward slide of the glass. She watched as it flew away.

She knew that just as the moth had been so close to freedom, she was so close to the answers that would set her free. The word *detoxify* came into her mind. She had heard of an energy healer who could oxygenate her weak blood. She had also heard of a center that supported resting, detoxifying, and helping to rid the blood of decades of toxic substances accumulated in the veins. Her fingers found the buttons on her cell phone, and she began to dial.

Adella's Story: Crashing, Burning, and Rising Again

The energy healer surmised that Adella had a malfunctioning thymus gland. It was no surprise to Adella that the gland regulating her body temperature was askew. She had been suffering through alternating waves of sweating and body chills for months. The healer performed the oxygenation and left Adella with a warning: "Do not attempt to detoxify now. Your body is not ready for it. To do so would cause all systems to crash." She added, "Your only chance to avert a crisis is to slow down and rest."

Unfortunately, Adella's impulsive nature did not allow her to heed this advice. Four days later, she checked into the detoxification center.

The first order of affairs was to give up the painkillers she had been put on for the rheumatoid arthritis. Hours into jaw-throbbing pain, she looked across the room at the telephone. "I can call 911," she said to herself, "and get pumped up with prednisone again, or I can ask for help."

When Adella had checked into the detox facility, she had encountered a lovely woman named Denise, who had come to write quietly and complete her third book on healing. Adella remembered having an odd sense of *knowing* deep inside when she met Denise. She sensed the strong, loving energy of a gifted healer. The minute they'd locked eyes, Adella had thought, "She is here for me." Denise was staying in the room across the hall.

It was 3 a.m., and Adella's heart was pounding in her head as she tapped on the door to Denise's room.

The door cracked open, and Denise knew there was no time to lose. She felt the rapid beat of Adella's pulse and the fever burning through her body. Denise and Adella held each other and called upon angels for help as fearful thoughts fired through Adella's brain. Two hours later, Adella's fever broke, and her pulse came down.

Adella returned to her room, but sleep eluded her. Hallucinations hounded her mind. She saw insects the size of monsters coming out of her intestinal tract. She prayed that angels would take away the demons inside her. And then she heard wings flapping. Her thought was of Archangel Uriel, and she heard him whisper, "Pay attention to your thoughts, as they are answered prayers."

The only way she made it through the night was with the archangel's loving guidance.

"Is this it?" she asked him. "Am I supposed to die now?"

"No."

"Is this unbearable pain my resistance to leaving?"

"No."

"Is this pain fire?" she questioned.

"Yes," she heard. "Fire."

A vision of a furious inferno formed in Adella's mind's eye, and she saw her addictions burning in the fire of her pain. Every addiction, from negative thought patterns to insidious eating habits, came forward to be devoured in the flames. The burning continued all night until she felt herself rise like a phoenix from the ashes. She went to breakfast in a wheelchair.

For the next few days, Adella rested—for the first time in years—and as she did, she accessed her inner wisdom. Her intuition guided her to a strictly vegan diet at the therapy center. As an alternative to cooking processed foods, Adella learned how to prepare raw foods that would energize her. The new way of eating promoted a cleansing and regeneration of the very cells of her body, and she was soon able to walk again.

Adella knew that her whole physical system of being had been compromised for most of her life, and now she was choosing to rest and heal her body. A new mindset emerged that made tending her health a priority. When it was time to return home, she committed to continuing to eat healthy foods and made exercise, followed by rest, a part of her daily agenda. Dealing with her anxiety around eliminating drugs and other toxic substances, like fast food, processed food, and chemically produced beverages, from her life was a continual mental and emotional battle, and making time for regular rest gave her the stability to cope with this challenge.

She was moved to sign up for a meditation workshop. She found meditation to be a rewarding rest practice and began discovering stillness within herself—the stillness we know when we quiet the outside world.

Today, nearly a decade later, Adella notices. If her energy begins to wane, she takes it as a sign telling her to get some fresh air, shift gears, or take a break. She notes when her body is rushing, and she honors its need to slow down and rest instead of continuing to push forward. With rest comes regeneration. If she starts to fall prey to an old habit and do too much, her body starts hurting. She notices when there is a twinge or ache that requires attention. She asks herself, "Why is the pain there?" Her body is now her intuitive instrument, telling her when rest is required.

She is also attentive to her thoughts; she examines each of her thoughts and asks, "Is this thought true?"

Adella's new pattern includes noticing emotional disturbances as well. In the past, she might shrug off her feelings, telling herself they were off base or explaining them away as overreactions. Now, by resting and going within regularly, she learned to trust her inner barometer. She has developed an acute awareness of when something doesn't feel quite right. Instead of rationalizing the issue, she stays with the feeling to look for a message and then acts upon that message.

Resting taught Adella how to be attentive to her body, her thoughts, her emotions, and her actions.

A Lesson Learned

Adella's story demonstrates how we can be seduced by the way of doing until we become disconnected from the clear warning signals the body is sending. Adella was mystified by the symptoms she exhibited. Yet it was not until her body broke down completely that she began responding to the critical need for rest.

Only in retrospect did Adella realize just how deeply decades of constant going and doing had depleted her. She had been physically, mentally, emotionally, and spiritually empty. In those rare aching moments when she had felt a tug at her heart, she would wonder what was missing in her life. Then she would return her attention to the demands of her everyday routine.

Adella had to learn firsthand how rest is needed to bring about recovery. After learning how to integrate rest into a healthy lifestyle, she was able to balance her multiple life roles—actor and performer, theater director and business owner, wife and mother—more effectively.

Her life has blossomed with the changes she's made. When she has rested, she is ready to embrace her projects with increased vigor. Rest renders her more prepared, present, and passionate to all her endeavors. Today, although Adella receives many opportunities to showcase her talent on stage, she is more discerning, choosing to accept those projects that she can balance with her need for proper rest. This shift in perspective that emerged from her experience has resulted in both improved performance and a more joyous life.

A Phoenix Rises, Renewed

In the year following Adella's recovery, I had the pleasure of being present on opening night as she made her debut in a full-scale musical. The show was a culmination of Adella's dreams and efforts envisioned over a lifetime.

As the house lights went up and applause thundered through the theater, Adella entered stage left. Her beaded red dress sparkled with a surreal glitter and flowed with palpable electricity as her feet glided across the floor. She moved across the stage with a complete command of the audience, and we were captivated by her charisma. She delivered her lines and belted out her musical numbers impeccably. At the end, her gleaming smile and shining aura were met with a standing ovation. When the curtain reopened and her co-stars had surrounded her on the stage, Adella took a well-deserved bow to a roar of applause. I clapped the loudest, as my heart was full of praise for her and her hard-won wisdom.

Exercise: Look into the Mirror

Is there anything about Adella's story that speaks to your life? Write in a journal about what aspects you can relate to.

Idea for Rest: Soothe Your Sweet Feet

Fill a tub or basin with tepid water and drop in your favorite scented salt or oil. Make certain you are seated comfortably and dip your feet in up to your ankles. If your feet are swollen from working or standing too long, consider adding baking soda, which is known to reduce swelling. Sit there for at least fifteen minutes and stay thirty minutes if time allows.

Afterward apply a soothing lotion to your feet and legs. Then lie down and elevate your legs on a pillow with your feet relaxed and pointed outward. Stay as long as you like.

In addition to providing rest, this practice will improve circulation.

CHAPTER TWO
The Seduction of Overwork

Constant activity and noise enervate the body and leave us feeling drained mentally, emotionally and physically.

Susan Smith Jones, *The Joy Factor: Ten Sacred Practices for Radiant Health*

Working too much has become an acceptable addiction in our culture. There are times when we mainline our work, as if it were a drug we must have more and more of even though it is taking us to the brink of burnout. Why? Maybe our self-esteem is often directly tied to our work accomplishments. Maybe we feel the financial pressure to buy into and maintain a certain lifestyle. Maybe we measure our success and happiness by what we do instead of who we are.

Whatever our reasons for overindulging in work, it is easy to disguise our addiction by giving it a different name, like "high productivity" or "a good work ethic." Such denial often compels us to not just maintain our addiction, but also reward ourselves for it—and the "rewards" we choose often become exercises in self-sabotage. We might find ourselves stealing moments to rush off on a shopping spree, which we justify by saying, "When the going gets tough, the tough go shopping." Feeling compulsive, we grab things we don't need or want. Then we see the balance on our credit card bill and berate ourselves for spending so much. Or maybe after working through our lunch hour, we come home starving and spend the evening eating an entire box of chocolates in front of the television. Then we beat ourselves up about how we overeat and need to lose weight.

Swinging between two extremes of overindulgence sets us up for a downward spiral of determination followed by deprivation, followed by a splurge, followed by self-punishment. The deeper the deprivation, the more grandiose the splurge, and the more grandiose the splurge, the more punishment we heap upon ourselves in the aftermath. If, in our determination to keep working, working, working, we repeatedly choose to deprive ourselves of rest and self-care, we will wake up one day and justify our splurges.

What we don't realize is that we are only countering our work addiction with another. We also don't want to acknowledge the real reason we indulge in any extreme behavior: to avoid facing our own inner emptiness.

The Pendulum Swings

The following chart lists unhealthy behaviors indicative of imbalance perpetuated by lack of self-care. When we hang out in the extremes, it is only a matter of time before our course is corrected. Can you identify a time in your life when you bounced back and forth?

Extreme 1	Extreme 2
Deprivation	Splurges
Denial	Overindulgence
Lack of self-care	Self-punishment
Sacrifice	Resentment
Overwork	Exhaustion
Overcontrol	Collapse
Despair	Euphoria

The Price of Overwork

Nora, a woman in my financial-planning office, would arrive early and leave late every day. One evening I went back to the office for a forgotten file, and I found her hovering over at her desk at 8 p.m. As I watched her shuffle a pile of paperwork, I remarked, "You may be able to work these kind of hours for a while, Nora, but you won't be able to work like this forever. Your body won't be able to handle the abuse long term. You might as well break the habit now before the habit breaks you."

Passing by her desk on the way out the office door, I asked, "Why are you doing this anyway?" Her response was a moot point in my mind. Whether it was to achieve more, earn extra accolades, or just to "get ahead," the price was too much to pay. Indeed, six months later, Nora's overworking proved an exercise in futility when she learned the company was being sold and her position eliminated. Even if she had been offered an alternate position, the new management would not have known of her long hours or given her credit for what she had done.

As we are swimming in our own overcommitment, the price we are paying is usually not that obvious. But make no mistake, there is a price. What is your habit of overworking costing you? Are you paying the price with your health? Is a meaningful relationship in your life being neglected? Are you giving up your spiritual practice? Whatever extra energy you are putting into your work is being stolen from some other area of life.

Are you willing to give up your addiction to work, stop the spiral of deprivation, and allow yourself to recover and rebalance? The choice to change a lifelong pattern is a courageous one. Yet this is the only choice you can make if you want to reclaim your physical, mental, emotional, and spiritual health.

Idea for Rest: Where There's Water

Spend some time near a body of water. Wile away an afternoon lounging on the beach or lingering alongside the lake. Even a local pond or swimming hole offers the opportunity to sate your senses with the liquid tonic of life.

A long, leisurely walk along the shore may prove to be the order of the day. Notice whether you want to gently submerge yourself, float about in the water, or go for a vigorous swim. Allow your instincts to take over. Perhaps sitting in the sand, silently observing the waves as they roll in, is all you need to calm yourself.

Bring a notebook to jot down insights that come to you during or after your activity. Record whatever comes to mind. Were you able to detach from everyday worries, or did thoughts of the proverbial to-do list plague your peace? Did you connect with the still voice within during your solitude? Where there is water, a well can be dug to discover fresh ideas. Write about any messages that may emerge.

CHAPTER THREE

Finding Your Barometer: How Imbalance Shows Up in Your Life

People search for their inner home in the wrong places: in professional success, material status, institutions, persons, pleasure and on and on. But none of these can ever be home. We end up spiritual refugees.

Sue Monk Kidd, *When the Heart Waits*

For most of us, the lack of rest creates a life imbalance. We feel off-kilter and can't quite identify what is causing life to be so out of whack. Discovering your barometer can be enlightening. Once your barometer gives you a reading, you can begin to take steps back to equilibrium. The barometer puts you on immediate notice. A barometer indicates pressure and measures change.

Many people consider signals in the body to be their barometer. But as we will explore later, the pressure must be very high before it will register in your body, and then it will register in serious, sometimes life-threatening ways, as Adella's story (chapter one) illustrates. It's better to figure out where the imbalance is through other early warning signs before it shows up in your body. The body should be the barometer of last resort.

I've observed that when I'm out of balance, a financial problem usually appears to get my attention. Since my business career has revolved around money, it probably isn't surprising that money is my barometer. This proved to be the case time and time again as I began building my business. When I was able to effectively manage client matters while honoring my own need for rest, the cash flow was unimpeded. If I was pushing myself too hard, the money flow would stop cold and stay cold until I got the message to slow down, take a breather, rest. At first this message seemed counterintuitive. If business is bad, shouldn't we be doing something, doing more, to change that? But doing something to get something just doesn't work for me anymore. Tuning in to myself and taking care of myself does.

Finding Your Barometer: How Imbalance Shows Up in Your Life

At one point, it was a game for me to go to my mailbox. If I was doing too much, I'd get letters offering all kinds of unpredictable excuses for why I wasn't being sent the money that was due me—everything from "the check got lost in the mail" to "we paid someone else instead of you by mistake." It was as if the channel from which prosperity flowed would become blocked until I stopped and took care of myself. If I ignored my needs, there would be no more financial support, no matter how hard I tried.

The reverse was true when I paid close attention to balancing my business activity with resting time. It was not unusual for thousands of dollars to unexpectedly and inexplicably show up in my mailbox when I was honoring myself as part of the natural flow of life. I'd receive an income tax bill that I did not know how I would pay, and a check for the same amount would show up from a source that I had completely forgotten about. My husband and I have often joked that we learned all our lessons from our bank accounts. A life balanced with action and time for reflection meant the cash would flow in and flow out without any hiccups. Whatever I needed would be there as long as I was there for myself first.

Our environments can serve as barometers as well. Working in the earth creates a symbiotic relationship with plant life. For those deeply connected to the earth, such as farmers and gardeners, the land will often reflect, like a hologram designed by the creator, where their lives have gone off track. They know that when the land flourishes, they are personally centered in the space that supports new growth—in every area of life.

A deteriorating living environment often signals trouble ahead. For some, this can mean a key appliance breaks down at an inopportune moment, a home sustains damage from an unforeseen storm, or the car battery dies. Our lives are composed of living energy, which connects our own energy with that of where we work and live. When something in our environment goes awry, that something is a signal. Whatever messages and issues may rise, the first steps toward addressing them is stopping and resting.

Parents might find that their children's behaviors are alerts telling them that they, the parents, need to rest. There is a saying I love to repeat when I see a smiling baby: "A happy baby means a happy mother." The reverse is also true. A fussy baby often means the caretaker is stressed and anxious, badly in need of rest.

Pet owners will often find their moods reflected in their furry little ones. It has been said that dogs take on the appearance of their owners over time. What is nary spoken of is how dogs take on the demeanor of their owners. Man's best friend can be a poignant barometer. My brother-in-law's beloved dog developed cancer during a particularly stressful period when my brother-in-law's business looked like it was going broke. Intuitively I knew the dog was carrying a message for him: he needed to change the way he viewed and reacted to his business concerns. Sadly, the dog died. Even more sadly, my brother-in-law was diagnosed with cancer a few years later and succumbed to the same disease as his dear dog.

Reflect on your own periods of struggle to discover your barometric pattern. What signs does life send your way to alert you that your life is out of balance? How do you know when you are leaking energy through effort instead of choosing the periodic rest that allows for life to flow in an easy, natural rhythm? Whether your barometer is your body or your bank account, knowing what to watch for can prevent a challenge from becoming a catastrophe.

A friend of mine was worried over the bills. Instead of doing more marketing for herself and her business to make more money, she took five days off to do nothing but rest. Can you imagine shutting down your email for five days? When she turned her computer back on, she had received twenty-two unprompted, unsolicited, paid speaking and teaching invitations.

The next time you notice your life's barometer is registering the need to give yourself the gift of rest, instead of trying harder to solve your problem, try one of the ideas for rest listed at the end of the chapters.

Signs of the Call for Rest

Feeling stressed is an obvious indication that we need to slow down and take a breath. Here is a brief list of common stress-overload signs. Which of them apply to you?

- I get frustrated easily.
- It feels like no one appreciates me.
- I am irritable and lash out at those I love.
- I can't seem to focus on what I'm doing.
- Routine duties are falling through the cracks.
- My thinking is muddled; I am confused and/or forgetful.
- There's not enough time for me to get it all done.
- I am exhausted at the end of the day.
- I'm not sleeping well.
- My body aches all over.
- There's no time for me to take care of myself.
- I fantasize about escaping my life; all my daydreams begin with "if only..."

Idea for Rest: Put on the Kettle

Put on the kettle and sit nearby while the water simmers in the teapot. Resist the urge to buzz about the kitchen as the water boils. Instead, be still and listen to the low whir and bubble of the water rising up before the whistle blows. Savor the process of making and taking your tea. Smell the flavor of the herbal bag and honey. The soft aroma rises to your lips until you let the sweet liquid heat the hollow of your throat with its fragrant splendor. Today, enjoy a cup of hot tea in silence.

CHAPTER FOUR

Signs and Stages of the Call for Rest

If you want to live a meaningful life that also makes a difference in the life of others, you need to make a difference in your own life first.

Cheryl Richardson, *The Art of Extreme Self-Care*

As human beings, we are comprised of body, emotions, mind, and spirit. The need for rest will affect us on all of these levels.

An early mentor of mine gave me a striking example of how a human experience evolves through the levels of reality: spiritual, emotional, mental, and physical. In other words, our experience begins in the spirit and moves into the body. This journey is clearly evidenced when a person makes the decision to take their own life:

1. The *spirit* dies first. A deep wound robs the spirit of the will to live.
2. *Emotional* suffering occurs.
3. The *thought* to carry out the act comes to the mind.
4. The *physical* act is carried out.

All of human life is played out in these four realms. The spiritual is the first level to give you a signal to rest. Sadly, many are caught up in commitments that preclude hearing the call of the spirit. When we don't heed the alert, negative emotions will set in. These emotions can range from anger laced with resentment to overwhelming grief. Today's label for emotional turmoil is "drama," and the second stage of upset comes loaded with situations sure to push your buttons.

If deep, dark emotions emerge and remain unaddressed, negative thoughts begin multiplying. Instead of immersing yourself in the joy of the present moment, you start playing the blame game. Long lists of everything you do for "them," along with all the times your efforts are going unacknowledged, start popping up unprompted. Dark, repetitive, unproductive thinking eats away at you.

A spiritual call unheeded and an emotional battering ignored, followed by endless unproductive thinking, inevitably leads to physical suffering.

The crash may come in the form of a collapse, as it did for Adella, or in a series of ailments over time, culminating in a deadly disease. Regardless, the pattern of physical deterioration is set in motion.

Forms of Rest

Rest is an effective tool for turning life around at any point in the four-level process. Any form of rest may be used to slow the process of entering into a negative cycle or put an end to the cycle entirely. Whether you choose to rest physically, emotionally, mentally, or spiritually, the act will resonate in all realms.

Spiritual Rest

Paying attention to your spirit is a good place to start when you find yourself descending into despair. There is no better antidote to anxiety than hanging out with your most authentic self. There are many paths to your spirit, including, but not limited to, prayer, meditation, writing in a journal, reading inspirational works, or sitting quietly in a sacred place, such as a church, temple, indigenous holy site, or cathedral. Nearly all methods require stopping or slowing ongoing physical or mental exertion as a precursor. Entering the realm of the spirit allows you to escape the petty cares of the ego and experience a sense of oneness with all that exists. Spiritual nourishment lends stability to emotions, serenity to the mind, and replenishment to the body.

Emotional Rest

Without some down time, our minds and our bodies become mired with the residue of emotion that often leads to illness. Prolonged anger or wallowing in pain depletes our energy, making it impossible for us to enjoy the good in life. An excess of unwanted or unprocessed emotion can leak out in an unhealthy and inopportune way. Intense emotions have a tendency to build until we're craving relief.

Take a break from overwhelming emotions by giving whatever you are feeling a rest. Instead of acting out, remove yourself from the situation, shift your attention, and focus on how to get your inner needs met. Once emotions are calmed and you are on an even keel, you are better able to discern the truth of your circumstance. When you allow yourself sufficient physical rest, anger or grief may rise to the surface as part of the natural unfolding. If so, resist the urge to stay stuck in an emotional quagmire. Allow these feelings to gently pass through and be released. Simply let the feelings happen.

Rest in a safe place where you can acknowledge your emotional upsets without getting caught up in them. The

How the Need for Rest Shows Up in Your Life

1. The spirit cries out in yearning for something more.
2. Emotions are strained.
3. Thoughts deteriorate.
4. Problems show up in the physical body, bank account, or surroundings.

key is to bring yourself back to the center of your being by softening internally. If you need someone supportive to talk the matter over with, vow to do that at a later time, and look to a trusted friend or contact a professional counselor to learn about tools for emotional clearing.

Mental Rest

The mind cannot conceptualize the completeness of a unified body, mind, and spirit. Completeness comes only when we learn to transcend the mind. Physical rest may take us further into our minds at first, but resting our bodies serves to transport us through our minds to what lies beyond. Only when we are willing to take that journey do we experience the fullness life has to offer.

Much has been written on how to interrupt the endless chatter of what some call "the monkey mind"—the never-ending mental story that seduces our attention and siphons off our energy. There are meditation techniques devoted solely to bringing us into the awareness that we are not our minds. Many use a mantra, a chosen phrase that is repeated until a thinking pattern is broken. Others recommend positive self-talk and affirmations. But true mental rest lies in the empty space between our thoughts. Learn to practice becoming aware of your thoughts when you are physically at rest. The moment just before you became aware of a thought, when there is no thought, is a moment of mental rest. Resting your mind in this way helps develop strong intuition and a connection with your innermost being. There, in the stillness, is a wellspring of divinely guided inspiration, what the mystics call "a deep sense of knowing."

Physical Rest

The natural flow of our physical performance improves with intermittent periods of physical rest. Our physical function is compromised without it. Scientific studies have proven the body needs rest to restore and regenerate at the cellular level. Deprived of this benefit, the body begins to break down. Ask any cocaine addict to describe the impact on her body resulting from constant stimulation. Anxiety, restlessness, loss of appetite, and insomnia take a toll, resulting in high blood pressure, malnutrition, and dehydration. In severe cases, damage to the heart and lungs can cause a stroke, heart attack, or even death. When we do rest, we enter a place of profound peace and initiate the transformative process of renewal.

Setting the Stage for Rest

The resting process is by its very nature experiential. The following simple steps create an unfolding within that cannot be quantified, only experienced.

1. Carve out time.
2. Go to or create a soothing environment.
3. Let go of responsibility to others.
4. Focus on the thought "It's my turn" or "I deserve this."
5. Be still.
6. Go within.
7. Listen.

1. Carve Out Time

Making time for rest begins with assessing your priorities. When you sense emptiness within and a yearning for what is missing, acknowledge that you must have time to attend to this call.

Next, review your calendar and commitments. Think about when you can put rest in your day or your week, and schedule it just like you would a client appointment or a kid's soccer game. Make a commitment to yourself and resolve to keep it, just as you would a commitment to your family or best friend. Remember, if you don't heed the call, you run the risk of eventually crashing. Recognize that there are long-term consequences of running on empty. Realize that everyone in your life will benefit when you are rested and refreshed.

2. Go to or Create a Soothing Environment
Can we find calm within chaos? Certainly the great masters were able to do so. But it is a lot easier to get calm, still, and stress-free when you are surrounded by serenity. Environment is a critical dictum in human development and often supersedes genetics in determining a myriad of factors affecting our states of mind and health. Use discernment when choosing *where* you will rest. Give some thought to the aesthetics that will cultivate the conditions of rest for you.

3. Let Go of Responsibility to Others
You may need to make arrangements for your loved ones to be taken care of during the time you devote to rest. Yet even with proper planning in place, your mind may wander into worry. If you feel you are responsible for others no matter what, you may need to practice letting go of responsibility that is not yours and accepting that

many circumstances are beyond your control. A belief that any outcome can be controlled is predicated on the illusion that all conditions are within your purview. Grant yourself a pardon excusing yourself from the responsibility of caring for others while you care for your wellbeing.

If thoughts of responsibilities plague your rest period, create a compartment in your mind to place them in. Pretend this is a special place for responsibility to wait in until you are fully rested.

4. Focus on the Thought "It's My Turn" or "I Deserve This"

If you have spent years performing tasks for the betterment of family or friends, the idea of taking a turn for yourself may feel awkward and unfamiliar. Focusing exclusively on the needs of others is a hard habit to break. If you are used to validating yourself through your acts for others and now choose to act for yourself instead, guilt or fear of unworthiness may surface. But remember: this is your time, and you deserve to be taken care of too. Use the phrase "It's my turn" or "I deserve this" as an antidote to any objections that arise.

5. Be Still

Those who are experienced practitioners of meditation will recognize the still point that resides inside of us. By

What Happens When You Rest

> Your body relaxes.
> Your mind stills.
> Your heart softens.
> Your spirit soars.

consciously stilling the body, we free ourselves to explore this stillness within.

Although constant stillness is not mandatory for achieving the state of rest, staying still is a good place to begin. Limit unnecessary movement by finding a position you are physically comfortable in for an extended period—much like you do when finding a good way to relax your body as you watch television or read a book. The key is finding a position that is effortless.

6. Go Within

Rest requires turning our focus away from what is going on outside us. Instead we are encouraged to focus on that which exists inside us. While you are resting, gently shift your attention and energy away from the world around you. Look with your mind's eye at the essence of you—who you are when the exterior no longer exists. Allow yourself to ponder your interior life.

Signs and Stages of the Call for Rest

The mind may be so full that the thoughts refuse to stop coming. As soon as you sit still and go within, distractions may surface. You may become aware of thoughts; the key is to keep from being attached to these thoughts, from making a mountain out of a molehill.

Allow your thoughts to pass through the mind as if you were viewing them on a movie screen, without getting caught up in the stories around them or making judgments about whether your thoughts are good or bad. Whatever comes up probably needs to be released. Give way to the process of letting thoughts go without resistance. Just keep gently redirecting your focus back to the still center within, the place away from where the mind resides.

If you continue to struggle with this process, consider exploring meditation techniques in order to develop a practice that allows you to disengage from your thoughts. Mindfulness meditation, Kriya yoga, and guided meditation are just three types of meditation that you may choose to explore.

7. Listen

We are all created by the same powerful infinite essence, and we all have access to divine guidance. Rest calls you to listen for that guidance. Once you have succeeded in creating a space between your thoughts, you will notice messages emerging. The messages you receive come from the spirit that has been stifled in years gone by. They may come in the form of new thoughts that are clearly not your usual mind muddle. Sometimes a message is audible, like a still small voice. Or it could be a hunch, intuition, or a knowing that does not require words to be expressed.

Listening to the spirit within requires patience and practice. Keep listening, and you will be given a lifeline for getting out of the frenzy of life and into the truth of who you are.

Life was meant to be lived from our highest level of being—spirit. With regular rest, you notice your life begins to flow easily and effortlessly. Relief comes and joy follows. Do "nothing," and you will become "everything."

Idea for Rest: The Sound of Music

Find a quiet place and put on some soft music. Steer away from any tune that stimulates and instead choose soothing sounds. Perhaps you relax best with the seductive sound of a flute or the sweet song of violin strings. You could also skip the music altogether and listen to a recording of gentle rain or rushing river water. Allow the sound to act as a magnetic force drawing you closer to tranquility. Imagine the light touch of angel feathers floating across your skin and feel the vibration caress your spirit. Stay here in the sound as long as you like.

CHAPTER FIVE
Permission Granted

What if it was your downtime, your lounging-in-bed-too-long time, your walkabout time, and your blow-Friday-off time that made possible your greatest achievements? Would they still make you feel guilty? Or would you allow yourself to enjoy them?

Mike Dooley, "Notes from the Universe," TUT (tut.com)

Think of a time you were given permission to have or do something special. Reflect on how you felt as you engaged in the activity. Did you feel validated? Safe? Appreciated? See if you can bring the feeling forward to today's circumstances.

When we give ourselves permission, we are agreeing to allow ourselves to receive. Permission is also an acknowledgement of worthiness. By allowing ourselves to acquiesce to the need for rest, we are the giver and receiver of our own blessing. We are both the benefactor and the beloved. These two qualities, giving and receiving, are interlinked in the natural flow of a healthy lifestyle. By giving generously, we spark the process of receiving abundantly.

Many of us who have spent our lives striving to please know how to give to others, but are challenged when it comes to receiving for ourselves. Women are especially wired to put the needs of others before their own—even to the point of detriment to themselves. But it is with sound reason that airline flight attendants remind us to put on our own oxygen mask before helping others put on theirs: taking care of ourselves is what gives us what we need to take care of others.

Declaration of Permission

Write a statement giving yourself permission to do or have something you value. Then read it out loud. Take notes on how you feel when you speak these words of permission. Notice whether you are able to receive graciously and embrace your own gift.

If you cannot, what do you need to explore further? What stands between you and permission? Is it a question of worthiness? Is it a question of guilt?

Use the exercise at the end of this chapter to uncover objections that come to mind when you consider giving yourself permission. Next to each item listed, write the fear behind the objection. Then ask yourself, what is the real fear? Be kind to yourself. Look over your answers and write the advice you would offer to a dearly loved friend.

When I explored my own objection to spending money on a manicure for myself, I uncovered an unhealthy need to have my teenage daughter depend on me. I told myself the dollars could be better used to buy things for her. In denying myself the treat I wanted, I held the misguided belief that I could control financial hardships that might befall my daughter. I had convinced myself that if I sacrificed my needs, my daughter would have her needs met.

Nothing could be further from the truth. In most cases, both parties to a sacrifice suffer in the end. What at first may appear a noble act often has unseen strings attached. The hidden agenda may come as a subconscious surprise. In my case, I was painting a picture of how I wanted my child's life to be instead of paying attention to how my own life was becoming.

I soon realized I was struggling with guilt and fear, and I was masking the need to let go of unfulfilled expectations. The time to focus on the needs of my child had passed; indeed, my daughter had become a capable adult.

The need for my own self-care had become paramount. Shifting my resources to care for my needs left me better able to support my daughter in a multitude of areas beyond financial. Example is a profoundly effective way to teach; I was showing her how a healthy woman takes care of herself and that I valued myself enough to spend time and money on personal grooming. Furthermore, my stance would give her the chance to grow in ways not yet imagined. As I focused more on my own needs, my daughter soon learned to make her way in the world without my help. Since I wasn't attending to her every desire, she learned self-sufficiency. Best of all, she learned how to discern and to take care of her own needs.

The antidote to my fear was to have faith and trust that I had raised a capable girl. I found I often wanted to protect her from feeling pain. But feeling pain was a natural part of her growing process. I had to give up the need to try to control my child's life circumstances. I needed to realize my role had changed from caregiver to cheerleader. Today my daughter is a mature adult who gives attention to self-care. She doesn't think twice when it's time to take a break from the stresses of her high-pressure job to treat herself to a pedicure.

A wise mentor of mine, Linda Starr, once conducted an experiment to decipher her own needs. At first she had to grapple with the guilt of taking time away from her responsibilities. The voice that whispered "Shouldn't you be doing something productive instead of lounging around all day?" had to be silenced. She began by giving herself permission to set aside a day to have no plans or to-do list. She called it "a pink dot day." A pink dot on Linda's calendar indicated a self-nurturing appointment. Her agenda for this day was solely to rest, listen to her inner yearnings, and respond in kind.

When the pink dot day arrived and she began to stir from her slumber, her first inclination was to go right back to sleep, which she promptly indulged. Upon waking a second time, she sensed her desire to put on a kettle of hot herbal tea. Then she parted the curtains to the window beside her bed and slowly drank in the view of the dawning day. Next she noticed a magazine beckoning her to flip through it and admire the glossy pictures on its pages. After she completed each activity, she would do what she coined as "checking in" with herself. Moment by moment she gave herself permission to listen mindfully to the needs of her spirit, emotions, mind, and body and answered the callings. In essence, she gave herself permission to spend an entire day doing nothing other than following her bliss.

The permission Linda bestowed on herself for one day revealed desires formerly buried beneath the busyness of the typical workweek. By allowing these needs to emerge, she honed her inner instincts. This later led to making lifestyle adjustments to better support her goal of building a successful personal coaching practice.

Linda summed up her experience by declaring, "If I feel guilty, I use the guilt as my cue to congratulate myself for noticing I am willing to do something for *me*. Then I give myself *permission*, give up the guilt, say my thanks, and enjoy!"

My friend Janet Conner, author of *Writing Down Your Soul* and the companion book, *My Soul Pages*, christens each new year by taking a "soul day" on the first day of January. Despite the pressing demands of her publisher and busy teaching schedule, Janet gives herself permission to put her activities on hold and have a sacred day of rest. As part of the permission process, Janet makes a point of acknowledging to herself and others the positive impact her soul day will produce.

After you have put together a permission statement specifically allowing you to receive rest and nurturance in your life, keep working with that statement until you have cleared out all objections that come to mind. When you can write the statement, resonate with the truth that springs from the message, and feel good about it, you are ready to receive your own reward. Challenge yourself to become a living testament to your declaration of permission to rest. Write about what this permission means to you.

Exercise: Declare Yourself

Write a Declarative Permission Statement
If you could give yourself permission to do something kind for yourself today, what would that be? The written word has the power to transform desire into destiny. Spend some time crafting a statement giving you permission to create the rest you need. Use words that resonate with truth for you and that encourage self-care.

Sample permission statements:

I, _____, give myself permission to take a nap today.

I, _____, give myself permission to spend an afternoon lounging on the beach.

I, _____, give myself permission to take a week off from work to nurture my soul.

Overcome Your Objections
What objection comes to mind when you read your permission statement?

After identifying your objection, ask yourself:

- What is the fear behind the objection?
- What is the real fear behind the objection?

- What advice would I give a friend or loved one who voiced this concern?

- What is the best antidote to the objection I can give myself?

Repeat this process for whatever number of objections arise. Keep rereading your permission statement and working through the objections until you can write out your statement and hear no objections. Then practice reading your permission statement out loud, to banish any doubt about worthiness and build confidence around the value of your intention.

CHAPTER SIX
The Science of Rest

*People are exhausted these days, though
they are often not sure why.*

Matthew Edlund, MD, *The Power of Rest*

Why rest when you could be doing something instead? The common misperception in our culture is that rest is a waste of time. But is it really?

Those involved in the medical field, closest to the front lines of physical function, have taken the initiative to explore what rest does or doesn't do. In *The Power of Rest: Why Sleep Alone Is Not Enough,* sleep expert Matthew Edlund, MD, refers to rest as "the original transformative technology." His groundbreaking work emphasizes the distinction between rest and sleep, explaining how they are two entirely different practices. Edlund says, "Active rest consists of directed restorative activities that rebuild and rewire body and mind." With tiredness and fatigue now common side effects of American life, he points out that "resting right can help you simultaneously feel fully alert and fully relaxed."

Edlund also explains that rest is one of the front lines of our infection-defense systems. It keeps our immune systems going. If we do not rest, our cells do not reconfigure, regrow, rebuild, and regenerate.

"Rest is as critical to life as activity. Rest aids survival, your pleasure, and your ability to find meaning in the world. In order to live well, we need to rest," writes Edlund. His research encourages us to do less yet expect to accomplish more, as resting fosters internal balance and health, increasing effectiveness. The key to effective rest lies in understanding how the human body really works and allowing its innate rhythms, cycles, and inner music to work for you, not against you. He poses the question, "If you could do less and become healthier, more productive and successful, would you? You can, if you know how to rest."

Stress-management expert Kelly Howell says, "Stress is not just a state of mind. It is a chemical state our bodies enter into with overwhelming challenge." Howell developed Brain Sync Brainwave Therapy, which offers subliminal programming to stimulate the alpha and theta brain states, which in turn promotes stress reduction.

The goal is to achieve total relaxation, refreshing body and mind. And if you regularly incorporate these resting techniques into your life, you can live stress-free forever.

Lissa Rankin, MD, author of *Mind Over Medicine,* believes that nurturing can "turn off the stress response in the body, elicit the relaxation responses known to induce positive hormonal changes, and return the body to its natural state of homeostasis which can induce self repair." Rankin promotes rest combined with optimism as the path to healing. She tells us the mind is capable of releasing chemicals that put the body in a state of physiological rest, controlled primarily by the parasympathetic nervous system. And when the body is in that resting state, its natural mechanisms are free to get to work on what's broken within it. In other words, rest allows the body to heal itself.

Lorrie Morgan-Ferrero, a professional copywriting strategist, promotes the link between rest and creativity. She says, "As a creative person, I can tell you sometimes a complete disconnect is the only way to stoke those innovative fires." To further support resting, she tells her fans, "You are *not* being lazy. Let go of the guilt. You are doing your mind and your work a great service by coming back to it refreshed with new ideas."

One could argue that the resting place acts as a portal to higher realms of creativity and consciousness. In those precious moments of nurturance, there is an intimacy with yourself that is an invitation to something more meaningful. There is the discovery of a clear connection between the vibrancy of the physical body, the creativity of the mental process, and the evolution of the spirit. True rest is an elixir and an antidote to the stressful life. Resting paves the pathway from stress to serenity.

There is a thread that runs through our humanness, much like a river runs through a valley. This thread connects the physical body, the emotions, the mind, and the spirit and acts as a conduit for energy. Resting allows us to grab onto that thread and gently ride that river. We move effortlessly down the stream of life, at optimum levels of living, when we give ourselves permission to rest regularly. This simple, sweet gift of love to ourselves lets our life flow.

What Is Rest?

As already noted, rest is a state of being that links body, mind, and spirit, turning us into an open vessel for receiving inspiration and restoration. What I am describing may defy definition, for rest goes beyond the height, width, and depth of the physical world into the core of our inner being. True rest gives the body a reprieve from physical exertion, cleanses the mind of thought clutter, uplifts the spirit, and replenishes energy.

As Tama J. Kieves points out in her groundbreaking autobiographical book *This Time I Dance!*, "Not working and resting are two different things." Rest is not lethargy. True rest is not loitering around devoid of energy. Rest is not characterized by acting like the proverbial sloth. Rest is not laziness. Lying in front of the television screen in the prone position may reflect laziness, but it should not be considered resting. In fact, it can be said that the lack of true rest results in all of the above. When you have truly rested in a profound way, your energy and zest for life are restored. If you have not experienced restorative rest, your inner yearning for it will cause you to be lazy.

Not all sleep provides rest. If we are unable to turn off the constant chatter in our minds, our night hours will be as fitful as our stressful days. Rest is far more restorative than sleep. True rest requires a release. It welcomes us into its womb, and we utter a sigh of relief.

In order to achieve a level of replenishment, we must cultivate the conditions for welcoming rest into our lives. Going within to cuddle close to ourselves is a process that requires preparation. Create the conditions, and rest will come. Here are some suggestions for doing just that:

Create a resting nest. A place of stillness will nurture rest. Stillness outside of you will soon create stillness inside of you. Where is the ideal place for you to achieve stillness? Can you carve out a corner with a comfortable chair? Is there a place in the yard to lay down a soft blanket on a spring day? For me, a porch swing was the ticket to traveling outside the business or busyness of my day. The soft brush of the breeze calms me and brings me to stillness as I swing.

Carve out time. Set the clock if you must, but be sure to give yourself over to the moment of rest until the clock chimes. This is your turn. This moment—this very moment—is all yours! During this time, let go of responsibility for everything and everyone except yourself.

Think about props. Surround yourself with whatever soothes you. This could be a bouquet of fragrant flowers or perhaps a lighted candle. Nature sounds can touch you in a place that has no words, and using an iPod with tracks of nature sounds may do the trick. Bring yourself a fluffy pillow or a silky blanket, a special talisman to touch, or an inspiring visual aid, such as a statue, carving, or a photo of a beautiful scene. Gather into your space whatever you perceive as conducive to rest. Let your senses lead you toward serenity.

Remember this: no rest is ever wasted. Every restful moment contributes to the quality of your life. When you emerge from a resting period, take note of any clarity, confusion, or creative impulses that may arise. Explore the diversity of your thoughts and feelings both before and after a time of rest by writing down your thoughts or perhaps by talking with a supportive companion.

If you think you don't have much time to spare, you may want to start out slowly when adding rest to your life. How about just fifteen minutes a week? Begin by taking baby steps. Once you experience the results and renewed energy added to your life, you will want to increase the frequency of resting periods until you discover your personal equilibrium. Ideally, rest will become part of your daily practice, like brushing your teeth and saying your prayers.

Exercise: Set Your Stage

Take a moment to list the conditions you want in order to welcome rest into your life. How can you set the stage?

Exercise: Signs of Being at Rest

Don't know how to rest? Visualize what an observer would see if they saw you at rest. In other words, ponder what you would look like if you were resting. As an example, here are ten signs that I am resting:

1. My phone is turned off.
2. I am alone.
3. My breath is soft and steady.
4. I am physically comfortable.
5. There is an absence of effort.
6. I am "in the moment."
7. My focus is on my own needs.
8. I notice beauty around me.
9. I feel peaceful and stress free.
10. My facial expression is serene.

Use this list as a springboard for creating your own.

Chapter Seven
A Matter of Time

Until you value yourself, you won't value your time. Until you value your time, you will not do anything with it.

M. Scott Peck, *The Road Less Traveled*

Visualize an experience that tantalizes all your senses at once. Let's conjure up the image of a romantic interlude. You enter the room where soft music is playing, and a bouquet of roses sends a glorious scent wafting in the air. Your lover takes your hand and gently strokes between your fingers, then gives you a glass of wine in an exquisitely cut crystal goblet. You admire the beauty of the light dancing on its edge as you bring the vessel to your lips and taste the full-bodied liquid. Your heart begins to open, and you know you are entering the space where blissful love resides.

In all this perfection, the one factor that can make this the night of a lifetime or blow the moment before it begins is *time*. Enter the evening knowing you have hours to revel in the arms of your lover, and you experience ecstasy. Enter harried and hurried, checking your watch and realizing you have to leave in fifteen minutes, and the experience escapes the moment you arrive.

Time is a man-made concept we can use to expand life or extinguish it. As our image of the romantic interlude illustrates, time is necessary to enjoy to the fullest what life has to offer. An allotment of time is today's treasure. This is a gift we must give ourselves at every turn.

How we choose to regard the concept of time is what frames our reality and makes our experience solid. Time is fluid and infinite. Yet the mind is capable of limiting our concept of how much time we have. What if we shift from viewing time as a restricted quantity to viewing it as an expansive quality? That new perspective has the potential to impact our lives in profound ways.

As a young financial professional selling my services, I learned that "not enough time" was a frequent excuse people used for not moving toward what would best support their lives. I also learned that excuse did not hold water. In most instances, they were lying to themselves. They bought into the belief that time makes their decisions for them instead of believing that they make the decisions for their time. Sales coaching taught me to view "not enough time" as a smoke screen. My job was to blow the smoke aside and reveal the real reason for hesitation, then talk about prioritizing. I would give clients a list of financial objectives and ask them to rate these objectives in order of importance. That simple exercise brought their values to the forefront of our conversation. Once they established that financial independence was a priority, the time necessary to commit to the financial-planning process became available. When someone says they don't have enough time for an activity they deem important, what they are really saying is that they don't value spending time on what they say is valuable. Reassessing both time and values will bring the true issue to the surface.

The steps to finding time to rest are no different than finding time for your finances or fitness: prioritize, plan, and schedule. Linda Starr scheduled pink days on her calendar, giving priority to providing time for herself (see chapter five). Ten years ago, I decided that Fridays would be personal days for me. I eliminated business appointments on Fridays and reserved one day a week to do as I pleased, with the stipulation that the day include some form of rest.

If you take a hard look at what is truly deserving of your time and energy, you will take the first step toward freeing up time for what you hold dear. This process may lead you to put boundaries around how much you can give to work, family, friends, and social causes. Giving yourself time to rest requires reducing time you now expend elsewhere. The ironic outcome is that the *quality* of time spent in each of those endeavors, which you may think of as stumbling blocks in the way of getting the rest you need, is actually enhanced. It's the simple law of supply and demand. Whatever is in limited quantity becomes more precious. Spend less time at work, and you will be more focused and productive when you do work. Spend less time with a certain friend, and you will be more present and engaged when you are together.

Take a moment to list your life priorities, from caring for loved ones to your vocation, and the percentage of your time that you spend on each. Where does tending to your own needs fall on the list? How much time do you allocate for rest? Are you spending your time on what means the most to you? Is there a project or a person that might benefit from less time?

Look at where you can spend less time in order to liberate more time to care for yourself. You may be surprised how reinvigorated you feel when you return to tackle those other tasks.

Drawing Boundaries

When you experience more resentment in your life than gratitude, more pain in your life than love, you may have broken boundaries. If you lose touch with your needs because you're so busy meeting another's, you may be giving too much. It sounds romantic to say you don't know where you end and where your partner begins, but in reality you are setting your relationship up for ruin. Giving too much creates an energetic pull between individuals where the giver and the receiver are out of balance and the gift becomes a bitter pill. You aren't doing anyone any favors by spending so much time giving your self and your time away.

Women who give too much often feel taken for granted when the receivers don't express appreciation. You will know when you have given too much time and energy to someone or something because you feel used up and like you are owed something in return, even if it's just a thank you. A true gift of your time requires no thanks, but receives thanks as part of the natural cycle of reciprocity that replenishes itself. The flow of giving and receiving is one of life's great paradoxes. When your needs are cared for first, you can give lovingly of your time without an unspoken agenda tucked inside your unconscious mind. That kind of gift feeds both the receiver and the giver. Furthermore, if you are giving too much time to others and not enough to your own care, you are not being true to yourself, your needs, and how you deserve to be treated.

Learn when to draw boundaries around an internal reserve that must be safeguarded and replenished. If you sense resentment building, take notice—that is a signal to start saying no to demands that will cheat you out of time to rest. Rest, love yourself first, and move forward only from that central core to begin giving time to others.

How does it feel when you know you have plenty of time? Do you breathe a sigh of relief? Do you let your guard down and relax? Do you find the task at hand flows easier with less mishaps and more enjoyment?

Do you find that when you are short on time, you are tense? Stressed?

Do you find yourself unconsciously sabotaging life by not giving yourself enough time to accomplish the task at hand or to enjoy the activity you have before you?

Take a look at the priority list you created earlier; notice how much time you are giving away to others. How could you make others aware of your need for time to yourself? How can you implement a revised approach to the benefit of all parties?

Melody swore that her six-year-old had radar to detect whenever Melody took time for herself. Young Emma would inevitably get out of bed and interrupt Melody's nighttime soak in the bathtub until they discovered recordable storybooks—books that Melody could record herself reading in her own voice. Now when bedtime comes for Emma and bath time comes for Melody, a pretty pink embroidered pillow that says "privacy please" is posted on the bathroom door. Emma knows that if she needs to hear her mom's voice when the privacy pillow is displayed, she is to return to bed and open one of her storybooks.

Explore what you think is keeping you from taking more time to rest by filling in the following blanks:

"I'd love to have more time to rest but _____."

"I'm not willing to take time to rest because _____."

How do these statements relate to the list of life priorities you prepared? Dig deeper by questioning the truth in each statement. What excuse are you using to keep from caring for yourself in a way that will keep you vibrant and healthy? Do you claim that excuse as your truth, or are you blaming someone else for your choices?

My friend Kathy complained that she could not rest because her husband always had a television blaring in the living area and master bedroom of their home. After careful consideration, Kathy chose to turn a quiet guest room into a yoga room. She installed her own TV on which she could play yoga DVDs or listen to calm meditative music. She created a cocoon where she could nestle in and rest. When her husband announced that he wanted to watch a sports event or war movie, Kathy welcomed the news as "found time" and used it to nurture herself in her new sanctuary.

One single mother I know with a thriving massage practice has a meditation application on her phone. If she finds her energy running low, she can choose a five-minute meditation to give herself a breather in between clients. When she has a client cancellation, she views it as bonus time for rest and tunes into a longer guided meditation with the touch of her phone.

Review your schedule for the past month. Is the time allocated to each area of your life reasonable? My sister once told me she was overwhelmed and couldn't find a minute for herself. I said, "Who is setting your schedule?" If you are giving too much at the expense of your well-being, see if there is something that can be shifted on your calendar to create more space in your life for rest.

Exercise: Give Yourself Time

Observe yourself when you feel time is of no consequence. Are you more connected with people and life around you? Do you smile more?

Ask yourself this: Am I willing to give myself some of my own time? How can I take more time for myself?

CHAPTER EIGHT
The Why

*I performed until there was no energy left to feel.
I stayed so busy that the truth of my hurting
and fear could never catch up. I looked brave on
the outside and felt scared on the inside.*

Brené Brown, *Daring Greatly*

Often we look at women of accomplishment and wonder, how does she do it? The real question is, *why* does she do it?

Refusing to look at what is driving you forward at a frenetic pace could result in a life crisis. Asking yourself why you feel you *have to* do something is the first step toward averting disaster.

Julie's Story

"When you lose your physical wellbeing, the truth comes forward. You are forced out of your head and into your body. It is your belly's way of saving your life."

Julie's words resound with deep insight and clarity, but they are not the words that began her story. Rather, they are part of the hard-won, unlikely treasure she has garnered on her quest for health.

Julie's story may seem like the memoir of a soldier who has braved many battles. She speaks of using a relentless, fast-paced lifestyle filled with achievement as a protective shield against an enemy lurking just beneath the surface. She speaks of the cells of her body knowing her whole historical identity. She speaks of ignoring her body's warnings to slow down, to take a breath, to take a moment. She speaks of how not heeding these warnings led to physical breakdown, emotional confrontation with her demons, and ultimately, a level of awareness that brought to mind the giant question mark she calls "The Why."

Julie's story began in rural Maine. She was reared in a sheltered environment she couldn't wait to escape. After high school, she took a job as an entry-level clerk at a local insurance company specializing in disability-income protection. Her long hours and dedication did not go unnoticed, and when the opportunity to leave the frigid East Coast came, Julie jumped at the chance.

The Why

A sales position at the insurance giant's Houston location gave Julie the freedom she needed to spread her wings and forge new frontiers, but it was not without struggle. She sometimes found herself, in the midst of a sales presentation, sitting across the table from a man that terrified her. She had a sixth sense for knowing when his mind would turn from sales to sex. Client lunches with him often included too many glasses of wine and Julie dashing for the door. It did not take long for her to begin piling on pounds, as protection from him and other potential predators. She often rationalized her behavior by saying overindulging in food and drink were just part of the job.

When Julie finally sought help for her weight, she had already developed high blood pressure and elevated cholesterol, and she was a borderline diabetic. Often her mind would become hazy after she left a client meeting. Periodic blackouts started to occur; she would wake up uncertain of the events of the previous night. She would work harder the next day, using her job to cover up her emotional pain. She set her sights on areas of life she could control—accumulating money, achievements, and high-profile sales awards.

On the advice of a friend, Julie applied for a well-known and frequently advertised weight-loss program. She was assigned a weight coach for encouragement, accountability, and overall support. Within a few weeks of working with the food plan, her weight-loss coach recommended she see a psychotherapist. The suggestion ignited a fury that rose up inside Julie's stomach and burned a hole right through her heart.

"I don't want someone lurking around inside my psyche. I just need a decent diet to follow," she told the coach. For God's sake, she thought to herself, who do these people think they are, telling me I need to see a shrink?

The coach gently persisted and explained that sometimes the best eating program in the world will not work if someone doesn't heal the emotional component of their eating habits. She explained to Julie that for every physical challenge we face, there is an underlying psychological issue.

Julie's coach also prescribed taking time off from work to rest, so Julie could give her body a chance to recover from her long hours. A break from the intensity of her high-powered job and the stress that came with it was what Julie needed. Instead, Julie resisted changing her lifestyle and pushed harder. She was looking for a quick weight loss and just wasn't willing to slow down, rest, and examine what was driving her compulsive behavior.

One day as Julie stormed out of the weight coach's office, she felt a burst of anger seeping through her pores onto the surface of her skin. Julie found herself shaking in a heated sweat as she began driving down the freeway toward home. Suddenly a black sedan seemed to appear out of nowhere and came within inches of sideswiping her vehicle. In a flash, the image of a stone wall rose up in the air and reflected off the glass in the front windshield. The wall was inside her mind, engendered by her consciousness, yet the scene looked so vivid, so real, that the sight obscured her view of the oncoming cars. She was compelled to pull her car over to the side of the road to catch her breath. As she did, the wall she saw in her mind began to crumble before her eyes. Julie gasped as she watched the stones tumble away to expose a tiny, fragile figure. There in front of her appeared the vision of a young girl subjected to abuse at the hands of a dark man. The girl was Julie.

Julie found herself face-to-face with the memory of a childhood trauma. The violence was as real as if it had happened yesterday. Overwhelmed and in shock in the days following the reappearance of the suppressed memories, Julie fell into despair. With the help of her weight-loss coach, she was admitted into a center for abuse survivors, with a diagnosis of depression.

Shortly thereafter, Julie became one of the statistics she had previously only read about while touting the value of purchasing disability-income coverage. "One in four individuals will suffer a period of disability before the age of sixty-five," she would say by rote in her PowerPoint presentations. In her wildest imagination, she never expected to be thirty-five years old and filing a claim for that very coverage.

The disability insurance policy paid Julie's bills while she entered the recovery period, which began with a thirty-day stay in a loving, supportive, therapeutic environment. The program gave Julie the tools to turn her pain into a path for growth. One of those tools was the opportunity to experience profound rest.

In her words, "The recovery center gave me the foundation, and the disability insurance policy provided the financial support. But I still had to face my demons. I finally understood my aversion to men, but I had to come to grips with the issue of my sexuality. Sexual intimacy with a man will never be possible for me. I'm not sure if the abuse I suffered is the reason why. It is a relief to give myself permission to explore the impact of my life experiences on my sexual preference."

Uncovering Our Inner Secrets

Often what appears to be a strong work ethic could be a cover up for suppressed memories of trauma or unresolved emotional pain from childhood. We sometimes fail to see how our American culture influences our ideas about accomplishment and self-worth. Low self-esteem could be an indicator of early life developmental trouble. Yet we tend to look outside ourselves for ways we can fill the void instead of looking within for our answers. The busier we stay, the less rest we get, the less likely we are to find the courage to face the real issues that need to be healed in our lives.

"Some women today feel they need to work harder than men in order to prove their self-worth," Julie says. "Staying busy was my mind's way of seducing me into believing I had to keep pushing myself in order to survive in the business world. My health issues forced me to stop the madness and ask myself what was really driving me on. There had always been a general sense of unworthiness lurking inside me, yet there was so much more buried there. The truth is, I cluttered my mind with busywork because I was afraid to let myself think about it. The root cause driving the low self-esteem was what I had to uncover."

Like many women, Julie found that while protection is often a priority, sometimes genuine strength can only be found at the core of our vulnerability. We must be willing to open up, to take a chance, and look at what has been covered up by life's accumulated baggage. We must wade through all the thoughts, the reams of experiences, that keep us from experiencing the truth. The act of hiding from what we fear could be closing our hearts and killing our souls. Simply resting is the key to opening the door to secrets that may lay buried in the psyche.

Once we uncover this subconscious sabotage, we have the opportunity to heal it.

Possible hidden whys are not limited to abusive experiences or sexual-preference quandaries. The mind is designed to insulate us from what we are not yet psychologically strong enough to bear, such as the memory of someone we love getting hurt. Even seeing someone we do not know experience trauma can create an emotional upset that enters our psyche and cripples us later. For example, we may go into shock as a defense mechanism when seeing a fatal car crash, only to have that memory surface sometime afterward.

Some women have to hit that wall even harder than Julie hit hers before they acknowledge the internal damage undermining their lives. One female minister summed up her own experience by saying, "After a series of unrelated operations, I realized I didn't have many more body parts they could take out. Was I just extremely unlucky, or was life sending me a message? Health confrontation has a way of putting you on a spiritual path. Thankfully, I listened to the call, or I would not be here to tell the story."

When asked how her trauma shifted her life, Julie speaks of a new set of values. "We often think we are striving for money or prestige, but we could just be running away from ourselves. It takes courage to ask yourself, who is surviving here? Is my self-worth surviving, or is my ego surviving? What is more valuable to me—my possessions or my peace of mind?

"Before the breakdown, I worked so hard and used career demands to foster my denial. I thought my weight and health were battles I had to fight. Now I realize my body became ill in order to support my survival. Today I view my weight gain and failing health as the gift that helped me find my truth; the gift that allowed me to rest and gave me back my life."

Anne's Story

Not all calls to rest come in the form of a health-care crisis. Like Julie, Anne entered therapy after uncovering deep wounds. She too used doing too much to avoid the sting of emotional pain.

Anne was an energetic wife, mother, and business owner leading a life that left little room for self-reflection. When the global economic collapse struck in 2008, Anne's oil-related service business took a big financial hit. The company hung on for a while until Anne's partner, a man she had long counted upon to hold up his end of the business, defaulted on a loan and declared bankruptcy.

"My partner was my original backer and handled the books. It looked like he began playing Russian roulette with our bank deposits," Anne recounted. "When he walked out the door, I was left behind to pick up the pieces."

A lump swells in Anne's throat whenever she speaks about what happened next. "Just when I thought it couldn't get any worse, my husband served me with divorce papers. I lost everything and everyone I believed in and trusted. My life's work was destroyed. My relationship was in tatters. My kids didn't know which way to turn. And I was dead broke. Life forced me to stop and rest. It was then that I knew I was no longer in charge. All I could do was surrender."

The truth was, Anne's marriage had been unfulfilling, but she had long turned a blind eye to the problem. She had stayed with her husband for the sake of the children and to keep up appearances. By burying herself in her work, she kept a safe distance from the dysfunction that had developed. She stayed busy instead of stopping to rest, because stopping to rest would have meant having to face the pain of a failing relationship.

As Anne discovered, those of us who have lived action-packed lives may find it difficult to shift into a lower gear.

"Life became a tug of war; the more life pulled me, the more I resisted. Time and time again, I had to let go of what I thought would always be mine to keep. The harder I struggled to hold onto the life I used to have, the more miserable I became. When I would finally stop and rest, my life would find a natural rhythm and a sustainable balance between activity and stillness."

Resting and mastering the art of letting go gracefully were the key skills Anne needed in order to begin living authentically.

Connecting Inner and Outer Lives

Anne and Julie are two examples of how inner needs can be masked by the outer circumstances of life. As both stories illustrate, we must find a way to stop the frantic pace before the frantic pace stops us. The quest to cope with what is out of our control begins with resting and shifting our focus within. Yet intuitively, we may fear what we will find when we do so.

For Julie, the secrets kept concealed in her subconscious mind sabotaged her life. Anne's fear of losing her sought-after success was realized. Rest often provides the path and fortitude to risk what can be terrifying to become transformative.

Julie's life looks much different today than it did before she came to grips with her suppressed memories. Following her recovery, she committed to a more balanced lifestyle that included work, social activity, and rest. She joined a softball team and a church, both of which contributed to a strong sense of community with other women like herself. Julie remarked that church was one place she learned to rest. The pastor included a meditative period as part of each program. It was there that Julie found her path for spiritual growth.

Today Julie looks back on her demons as damsels in distress who were calling her to feel and address her inner pain. Once she answered that call, she saw a marked improvement in her health, attained a manageable weight, and began pursuing a same-sex relationship. You could say Julie is well on her way to finding authentic happiness.

Exercise: Finding Your Way

Why do you have to keep up the hard pace? Discover your whys by finishing the following questions:

The subconscious pain I'm trying to avoid is _____ .

If I'm honest with myself, what I'm really afraid of is _____ .

The root of the core issue is _____ .

The deepest part I have to deal with is _____ .

Idea for Rest: Splurge in a Soak

Now is the time to lock the bathroom door and light the scented candles. Let your favorite sweet aromas fill the air. A good bath feels like going home to the waters of the womb, where you can feel safe and serene.

Another option is to immerse yourself in a favorite swimming hole, where you can feel the wind in your face and taste the savory flavor of salt in your mouth.

Wherever your ideal spot is, be it in the wild throes of a waterfall or the intimacy of a tiled tub, indulge in a long, fragrant soak until all your senses are sated.

CHAPTER NINE
Pushing Through

When we fill the stillness with too much doing, we are often trying to outrun our sometimes unconscious conviction that who we are will never be enough, the things we try to hang onto—our work, our relationships, our reputation and perspective—are the things we believe will make us worthy of life and love even though we fear we are basically and inherently flawed.

Oriah Mountain Dreamer, *The Dance*

What is the price you pay for pushing through? Have you ever had a time in your life when you did everything right and life still went all wrong? Good intentions aside, circumstances can go awry. Despite best efforts, sometimes you are sabotaged when you least expect to be. "Just do it," you hear in your head, and you do, even though your heart is crying "I can't do it—I just can't do it anymore!"

There are passages in your life where you simply need to take time to reevaluate your life and your values and give yourself a break instead of pushing yourself to the breaking point. Unfortunately, Western culture condones rest only for specific reasons. It's as if society expects you to push through internal challenges or those challenges that fall outside the norm without taking time for rest. As a result, when your spirit is aching to the core, your wake-up call will often come in the form of a life circumstance that your family, friends, and social circle will deem an acceptable reason for rest, such as . . .

- Illness
- Surgery
- Injury
- Giving birth (a brief respite only)
- Death of a loved one (although you are still expected to be there to greet and serve guests during the initial time of grieving)

One of my early mentors used a traffic-signal analogy to explain a warning system with which we are wired. When you start down the wrong road, you will see a yellow light flashing. Should you choose to ignore the yellow light, you will see a red light. Should you choose to race through the stoplight, you will inevitably hit the Mack Truck. You will hit the Mack Truck head on. Then, whether you have any fight left in you or not, you will be forced to stop—and rest. Too often, society pressures us to ignore the warning signs and tells us it is not acceptable to stop until the Mack Truck forces us to.

Many of us do not realize how much our collective view of resting and habits of not resting are based on external cultural messages. How many times did you contribute (albeit unconsciously) to creating these "reasons" for yourself by pushing through? What is the price you paid for pushing through?

My friend Jeanine thought she could be all things to all people. As a psychotherapist, she often carried the weight of her clients' mental health problems on her shoulders. The mother of a daughter dealing with alcoholism and the wife of a demanding husband left Jeanine little time to rest. It seemed she was surrounded by pain. Life was giving Jeanine signals to stop and rest in order to be able to address what life had handed her. But Jeanine pushed through her days, believing that if she could just get through this rough patch by doing a little more for those she loved, everything would be OK.

Nothing could have been further from the truth. When Jeannine landed in the hospital with pneumonia, she realized she was no longer willing to pay the price of her health. Pushing through had simply cost too much.

Reflect back on your life. How many times did you ignore the warning signs to slow down and instead pushed through anyway? Why did you do so? What would it look like to make time in your life to rest before a trauma has befallen you? How can you learn to listen closely enough to hear the whispers of your heart before the damage is done?

Exercise: What Are Your Warning Signs?

Have you discovered your barometer? What do your warning signs look like? What do your yellow and red lights look like? Do they come in the form of an upset with a loved one? A mishap at work or a lost project? Journal about the times you ignored life's wake-up calls and pushed through anyway. How can you heed the warning signs next time?

Exercise: Who Is Pushing You?

Who will support your self-care when you see the warning signs? Is there anyone you should stay away from because they will push you harder?

Think about who is pushing you and how that pressure impacts your ability to rest. Are you willing to stand your ground and put yourself first? How can you respectfully make your needs known and draw your boundaries? Are you hanging onto relationships that deplete you, even though they are not really your responsibility and need to be let go?

Exercise: Let Go

Close your eyes and see yourself letting go. Tell yourself you are giving up everything and everyone you are trying to keep up with. Let the act of release sweep over you like a tidal wave rushing onto the shore. Say to yourself, "This is it. The struggle is over." Sigh with relief and surrender. Listen to your chest heave as the fight is expelled from your lungs, bringing the tranquil moment you have longed for. You can almost hear the heavy burden you have been carrying land outside yourself with a loud thud. What is left behind is what is real, what is true for you. What is left is the sweet silence of all that is and all that ever will be. Rest there in the palm of the universe.

I wrote the following poem while pondering the push and pull of daily activity that so often consumes time and leaves us wondering where life went.

A Life Was Lived

It would seem
that somewhere between my morning shower
and slipping on my bedtime robe at night
a life was lived.
Between that magical moment when night becomes day
and the sun touches the earth at dusk
memories were made.
There were gestures and emotions
finding their way across the room,
questions upon questions
met with fleeting wisps of knowledge,
of feeling safe for a second
and then floating away.
As I search for the evidence,
a freeze frame could not catch my life.
Yet it was there—wasn't it?
Alongside the lake at my grandmother's house,
walking and humming to myself,
holding my newborn daughter in a hospital bed,
watching as she drew her first breath.
The mystery unfolded somewhere.
Perhaps it was a secret nook deep inside my heart,
or maybe in the spaces between the lines of an open book
all the while it lay upon my lap.
It would seem a life was lived

buried beneath the bills
and the business decisions.
Shaking my head at a ridiculous notion.
Gritting my teeth behind a broad smile.
The times I was caught laughing at myself
or crying for no reason,
wondering who would ever love me,
then learning how to love myself.
Where did it all go?
It all means so much
just before it disappears
like a shrinking violet
imploding all of its glory
leaving you wondering
a life was lived, was it not?

Chapter Ten
Giving It Up

There's a saying in France, "Know Thyself." Not enough women take time to sit down and figure out what will give them balance between work, family and life in general. And women have to learn—don't try to be Superwoman. Take a few hours off. We women want to control everything. We don't want to delegate. But sometimes, you just have to let go.

Miereille Guiliano, author of *French Women Don't Get Fat: The Secret of Eating for Pleasure*, in a *Houston Chronicle* interview

What would you have to give up in order to rest? Do you think that in order to rest you may have to spend less time with your spouse, children, friends, or business colleagues?

Ponder this: what if you knew deep down, where only the truth exists, that your time with loved ones would be richer, deeper, and more rewarding because you rested? Entertain this possibility. What if a rested, energetic person would contribute to and enhance the lives of loved ones more than a tired, depleted spouse or mother? What if respecting your own needs led to receiving more respect from your family?

Perhaps we have been conditioned to wait until we get a sign from above, until certain things fall into place or the stars align perfectly, before giving ourselves permission to pay attention to our needs. In fact, the opposite is true. Once you commit to yourself, the world rushes in to support you. Make a clear choice, and all kinds of synchronicity will show up in your life. The manifestation arises from the commitment, not the other way around. The universe hears your call and responds.

To rest more, you might have to work less. Are you thinking that if you worked less, your finances would suffer? So did I at one time in my life. As an experiment, I worked with the affirmative statement "The less I work, the more money I make." This phrase became my mantra when I stopped going to the office on Fridays. That was in the 1990s. In looking back, I see that by reducing my hours at work, I was more present and focused during work-devoted hours. As a result, I increased my productivity. My mantra became a magnet for more money.

Giving It Up

What if stopping to rest was the only daring step you must take to discover a priceless new source of income? Would you be willing to take that chance? If the answer is yes, you may arrive at the place in life where income is created from more than one source—what Tama J. Kieves, author of *This Time I Dance!: Creating the Work You Love*, calls "multiple income streams."

When my children were small, they would frequently ask for something new. Maybe it was a new dress or toy. If they were thinking big, it would be a bike or new bedroom. To help them fulfill their desires, I would help them make vision boards. We would set a time to gather and write about what we wanted. Then we cut out pictures from magazines with images representing our heart's desires. The last step was making a list of the different ways the money to obtain our vision could be sent to our family's bank account. For example, my husband or I might get a raise, a bonus, or overtime pay. Maybe the funds would come from an unexpected gift or inheritance. "How about a lemonade stand!" my little ones would exclaim. "Or selling baked cookies?" I would nod in agreement. "A part-time business endeavor may be just the answer we seek. Or maybe a good investment," I'd explain. Then there was their dad's all-time favorite possibility: hitting the lottery. You have to give up the limiting thoughts and beliefs of what is possible and look to creative avenues for your desires to materialize.

There are more opportunities today than ever before in human history. Newly created professions and income sources arrived with technology. One could venture to say that an Internet business is created every waking day. Yet for ideas to emerge, one must have the space in life to connect with these ideas. If we fill up our lives with to-do lists and leave no time for chance opportunities, we will never notice the doors that are opening all around us. What is behind your door number one? Number two? And number three? When we give up our attachment to how we think life should be, life has a way of bringing us lovely surprises in the form of new experiences and creative ideas.

Here is a tough idea I had to overcome: to take time for yourself, you might have to give up being a selfless martyr. Resting smacks of self-indulgence. It seems to border on greed, this act of giving to yourself. What will your loved ones think has become of you? Worst of all, you may have to let your guard down and give up controlling everything.

It has been said that control is the ultimate illusion. No one among us can truly control the world around herself. Yet we suffer under the spell of this impossible ideal. When we stop struggling to hold onto the delusion of being in control, life can unfold gently, and there will be no need for a dramatic wake-up call to get our attention. Unless we voluntarily give up, a tragedy, illness, or

Giving It Up

accident will eventually force us to give up. That's when we become a candidate for collapse. What if you give up the idea that you are in control instead of buying into that illusion? What if you chose self-care instead of letting yourself crater?

What if the simple act of making time to rest became a part of your life? What if you could take all the time you needed—an hour, a day, a week, a month, or a year? What would you have to give up to make time for the rest you need?

If the only thing you had to give up in order to rest was your own thinking on the matter, would you be willing? So often we get filled to the brim with thoughts that cry out in urgency, as if it is imperative that we engage in their dance. To pull away from the seductive thought movement of the ego-based mind can be a tireless task. Could you tell yourself, "Your thoughts are not necessary. Go back where you belong. You have no power over me!"

Rest is entirely experiential. Our needs vary, but you will know if you have rested enough by the level of health and energy you experience afterward. A telltale sign that you have received the rest you need is a renewed zest for living. Only you will know when your zest is fully renewed.

Visualize giving yourself permission to rest for as long as you need. What do you look like? What do you feel like? What new ideas have emerged? How have you changed?

Practice saying to yourself, "All I have to do today is breathe out and breathe in."

Idea for Rest: Breathe

Allow your breath to flow freely as you read the following words:

> Let me sit, if just for a moment, and breathe,
> to allow my breath to take me from the inside out.
> Breathe out.
> Breathe in.
> Breathe out my fears and anguish.
> Breathe in goodness, safety, and nurturance.
> Breathe out the toxins trapped in the cells of my
>   body.
> Breathe in vibrant health.
> Breathe out my tension and worried thoughts.
> Breathe in the blessings of the earth and the sun.
> Breathe out anxiety.
> Breathe in serenity.
> Let me remind myself that the only thing I must
>   do today is breathe—
> just breathe.

Chapter Eleven
Facing Fear

It is the mental arena that most takes us into fear of the future, worry, angst, and anxiety, and cuts us off from our own deep wisdom, optimism, and hope. How best may we stay in hope? Not, I believe by thinking our way to it. Hope lives in the wisdom of our hearts, arms, legs, and feet.

Justine Toms, *Small Pleasures: Finding Grace in a Chaotic World*

What fear do you have to walk through to rest?

In a weekend workshop, I learned a new meditative technique that resulted in a profound state of physical rest. But as my body unwound, my emotions wound up. From the pit of my belly I felt the heat of anger rise. It was as if a fierce wolf had been hiding in a dark crevice deep inside my gut. Searing emotions coursed through my veins. After years of blocking out my fears, the wolf came home to haunt me. It was as if every pent-up emotion I had denied having was making itself known at once. The deep, guttural howl of the wolf burst me at the seams. An outlet was open. The wolf was being set free.

This meditative rest could have been comfortable, but instead it unleashed my fears. Deeply restorative rest would not come until I answered the call to face the hidden fears that I had never before been willing to acknowledge.

The first fear I noticed was the fear of failing financially. It was lurking behind my professional veneer. Dying broke would be a devastating blow to my long-standing career dedicated to money management. I feared not living up to the expectations of my family, business colleagues, clients, and friends. Incompetence seemed a mortal sin.

My most fervent fear was the fear of losing someone I love. Someone I held dear might pull away from me and break my heart. Or worse yet, a loved one could fall prey to harm on my watch.

During the weekend workshop, I learned to welcome each fearful thought my mind drew into my experience. I viewed my fears like a detached observer would, seeing them almost as if they were part of a plot projected on the screen in a movie theater. I spoke softly to my fears to soothe them. I imagined stroking them one by one on their underbellies and sighing, "Is this what all the fuss is about? Come here and sit in my lap so I can rock you in my arms." A shift in my perspective was created through love and humor. Yes, you could say I would humor my fears. I also loved and humored myself, delighting in the discovery that fear dissipates in the face of love and laughter.

There is a connection between letting go of your fears and your ability to rest. Until you are willing to acknowledge what you are afraid of, fear will sabotage the sweetness in your rest experience. Rest opens you to release anything that is holding you back. Even fears you are not consciously aware of may come up. When they do, resist the urge to fight them off or to judge yourself. Allow whatever fears arise to pass through your being unencumbered.

You can also write about your fears. Keep a pen and pad close by, and if fears rise up during your rest period, write them down to revisit later. Tabling the fear for the time being will allow you to welcome the rest you need and deserve in the moment. What fears have you been resisting or hiding from? What fears may surface if you rest? How will you cope with facing your fear?

Remember that the words *scared* and *sacred* are close cousins. Can you think of a circumstance when being scared led you to something sacred?

Idea for Rest: Heart Meditation

Find a quiet place where you will not be disturbed. Sit comfortably, close your eyes, and become aware of your breathing. Draw a deeper breath; feel your abdomen gently expand and contract. Continue this deep breathing for a few minutes until you become relaxed.

Focus on your heart for a moment. Allow yourself to feel the love in your heart. Visualize sending this love from your heart out into the open space of your world, your universe. Now visualize the love returning to your heart. Do this a few times until you feel the flow that feeds life going through your heart, out and in, in and out.

Now think of something you are afraid of or have feared in the past. Surround this thought with the love emanating from your heart. Then think of the opposite of your fear—fearlessness in general or the ideal outcome of a fearful situation. Send love from your heart to this thought as well. Notice how these thoughts exist separately from you.

Challenge yourself to go past both the fear and the fearlessness to a place of oneness, where outcome is no longer an objective. Send your love far beyond the horizon to this place where separation does not exist and endless peace resides.

Finish by drawing the love back into your heart until your heart is full of loving energy. Rest here until you are ready to open your eyes.

CHAPTER TWELVE
Valuing Yourself

*We are all born with an uncanny sense that is our
interior Self that is our most valuable, our most
powerful treasure. How well we refine this inner
power determines whether the external crises of our
lives will "make or break us," as the saying goes.*

Carolyn Myss, *Defy Gravity*

What would you have to value in yourself in order to rest?

When I look back, it seems like redirecting my life was somewhat like turning around the *Titanic*—nothing short of a monumental task. I had over thirty years of full speed ahead, with all the trimmings, including industry meetings, solid-color suits, and endless hours mulling over markets and mutual funds. My activity and energy I was expending was meant to bring in more business, more success, more stuff. Stopping what I was doing was like trying to bring a massive money machine to a halt, while at the same time not threatening the life of the goose that lays the golden eggs.

Eventually my choice to stop came down to valuing sanity over security. I had to learn to value myself for something other than my accomplishments. I had to place value on attending to my own needs. I had to believe I deserved reward for doing absolutely nothing, yet being everything I am. Lastly, in order to approve of myself, I had to risk losing the approval of others.

A dramatic shift such as this is not without upset, chaos, and loss. It requires faith, prayer, and the power of grace to stay with it. Giving your internal needs attention is not without its own form of challenge. There may be days the doubt creeps in, insidious devil that it is. "What a waste of time this resting is," your inner critic may growl. Perhaps doubt's accomplice, apathy, will show up. Those are the moments when you shake your head and say, "What is the use?" You may even encounter unexpected grieving for the way you used to be able to "do it all" and feel satisfied with a life of outward achievement.

There was a time when I was a master at ignoring the gnawing that had begun in the pit of my stomach. Then the day came when I drove to the office that once held so much promise, and it dawned on me that I downright dreaded going inside. That candle had already been burnt at both ends. A life of placing value only on assets or activities with dollar signs attached was surely coming to an end.

Today what I value looks very different from what I coveted in the past. Instead of reading a financial statement, I prefer to read a good book with a meaningful message. Inspiration has become my currency, and I spend it wisely. No rest is wasted. Life organizes itself around my priorities. My top priorities are self-care and spiritual growth, followed closely by the connection with my husband of twenty-five years. Relationships matter the most to me now, the most significant one being the relationship with my authentic self. Taking time for me has translated to new possibilities, creativity, and unexpected sources of revenue.

Exercise: Inventory Your Values

Take a few moments to write about what you value. Looking back at your life, can you see the evolution of your values? For example, what did you value most as a teenager, as a twenty-year-old, at forty or fifty? What precipitated a shift in values?

What are the characteristics you most admire in others? For example, do you value honesty or compassion?

How do you embody these qualities? Are you capable of valuing the act of treating yourself honestly and with compassion?

Make a list that reflects your values. Use the questions in the paragraph above to get started. Contemplate how to place value in and enhance your life with what means the most to you today.

Idea for Rest: Linger and Lounge

Is there a place where you always feel rushed even though your heart wants to linger? Left to our own intuitive inclination, most of us would stop and smell the roses more. Block out an afternoon to linger in an antique shop, local nursery, or rural setting. Anywhere you have wished you could stay longer qualifies for this outing. Move the focus of your attention away from any specific achievement or result. Instead savor each step, allowing yourself to linger as long as you like. Imagine you are freeing your awareness to go where it will.

When you return home, find a good spot to lounge in. Maybe you have an outdoor patio or a quiet corner in your living area that calls to you. Gather up some old magazines or a pile of photographs and flip through them, noticing the visuals that capture your attention. Perhaps you can put some images aside to make a collage. Perhaps what intrigues you will show you something new about yourself, but defer any structured activity for a later day. Vow to give yourself this special time to do nothing but linger and lounge.

Dream on the Beach

I had a dream on the beach.
I saw myself from afar. . . .
I was in a delicate flowing dress.
There was a beautiful glow about me.
I reached out a hand to myself.
I was just out of my own reach.
And when I took my hand,
we began to dance.

It was a beautiful dance.
It flowed so naturally.
My heart was filled with love for me.
How gentle, poised, how agile I was,
so full of peace and joy,
so utterly radiant.

And when the dance was over,
I became filled with happiness deep within.
How very special it was
to share this moment of closeness with myself.

CHAPTER THIRTEEN

Margo's Story: Healing from the Inside Out

*Our highest calling in life is precisely to
take loving care of ourselves.*

Erich Fromm

The shamanic healer took a step backward after entering the room. Margo lay waiting on the treatment table at a renowned resort in northern Arizona, known for pampering its guests. After a year of struggling to heal illness through diet, alternative therapies, and prescribed rest, Margo was waiting for confirmation of her hard-won progress. Instead, she was met with a shocking pronouncement.

"Your body and your mind are in a huge battle," the healer said. "Your body wants to rest, but your mind keeps telling your body to go, go, and go. Your mind is holding your body hostage."

Margo's physical body had become totally disconnected from her feelings and her spirit. As a result, her energy had become toxic—so toxic that the healer wanted to flee the room.

Margo had been seeking rest, but could not get her mind to release the demands on her body. In the words of her physician back at home, "She had rested, but she had never let go." Little did she know just how much she would have to let go.

Born into a powerful legacy of accomplishment, Margo was the granddaughter of the first female marine and the youngest daughter of a financier. Both her father and mother were graduates of prestigious colleges. Raised in Manhattan, Margo attended a private school with stringent standards and fierce competition, and she sought to keep up with her two older sisters, who excelled in academia. Years later, Margo's mother told her that when Margo was in the fourth grade, she had been told that her third child would never reach the same level of achievement as her elder daughters. To her mother's credit, she had looked the bearer of this news straight in the eye and said, "I think you're wrong." Margo felt deep appreciation for her mother's belief in her ability, but

Margo's Story: Healing from the Inside Out

unspoken implications of her mother's message ignited in her a lifelong desire to achieve.

In college at Harvard, Margo danced, figure skated, coproduced a skating show, helped start a women's hockey team, wrote her thesis, and graduated with honors. While skating and dancing, she relished the joy of connecting body and spirit. Through musical interpretation and physical expression, she found an integral piece of herself.

After college, Margo landed a job at ABC Sports. As a production assistant to the best signature figure skating director in the world, Margo entered a male-dominated career with a mentor who set the bar high.

"Everything about television is about proving yourself," she shared. "My boss would speak with bravado of his fourteen-hour workdays. In TV, your stamina gave you your bragging rights—never mind if your body was crumbling."

Margo was passionate about her work and quickly rose to the top of her profession. She became a director/producer, savoring the opportunity to direct beautifully lit and choreographed exhibition shows, along with the brilliant, competitive performances of gymnasts and skaters at four Olympic Games.

When Margo met her husband-to-be, she was thriving on the adrenaline of the world of television. Three weeks into a whirlwind romance, he proposed, and she accepted. Within a year, her spouse was offered a position in Texas as a TV news reporter. Still in her twenties, Margo had barely settled into their modest home in the San Antonio suburbs when her two stepdaughters, ages eleven and thirteen, moved in.

Margo answered the call of caring for her stepdaughters, but did not give up the career she considered her calling. When she gave birth to her own daughter, Rachel, she went back to television four months later. Margo broke through barriers for "working remotely" by preparing for events in Texas, then going on site to the sporting events and returning home to piece together the editing. Gifted with a meticulous eye for detail and intense focus, she often was at event arenas until 3 a.m. for camera blocking and then went back to the arena at 8 a.m. for rehearsals before taping late into the night.

Margo lived for the moments she made magic on screen. "Five seconds to camera, number two, tight face," she would say. She experienced a thrill when the camera angles conveyed stunning shots full of drama, color, and artistry.

With eight years of freelance directing and four Emmys under her belt, Margo presumptuously prided herself on being able to get more done in one day than she thought anyone else could. She juggled family and job, living the delusion of being unstoppable. In reality, oftentimes she was not living her life, but just surviving

Margo's Story: Healing from the Inside Out

it. Those around her wondered how she did it all. Looking back now, she wonders also.

Excellence in Margo's line of work required doing her homework, boldness within the moment, and learning to trust her instincts. Yet when her body sent signals for help, Margo denied them. She returned home from a month-long assignment at one of the Winter Olympics with a raging respiratory infection. Margo's answer was simply to power through. After all, she was the Energizer bunny and never got sick. Surely she would simply "snap out of it" once she had time to recover.

But for the first time, she hit an insurmountable wall. Margo's two most coveted assets, high energy and clear focus, gave way to debilitating, ongoing fatigue, along with clouded thinking. It reached a point that some days all she could do was drop off and pick up her daughter at school. Even the simplest chores, such as grocery shopping, became so exhausting that she headed straight home to bed.

Western medicine failed to tell Margo what was happening to her or how to change it. In desperation, she turned to alternative therapies, leaving no stone unturned in her quest to determine why she felt so depleted. Following months of misdiagnosis, a unique health care practitioner, who combined both Western and Eastern healing philosophies, found that an illness known as candida was causing high levels of yeast to spread through Margo's body, overtaking good bacteria and weakening her immune system. A rigid regimen, including a diet free of sugar, yeast, and dairy, with daily herbal supplements was prescribed. Margo dutifully followed the protocol, but also continued to drive herself on by accepting work assignments that pushed her past her limits. This failure to heed the warnings relayed by her body resulted in severe adrenal fatigue.

Weeks later, when her physical health had fallen even further, her frustration led to following up on a hunch to test her home for toxic mold. The results confirmed that mold was present. Even though it was a relief to discover that this additional element was a key contributor to her decline, Margo was completely overwhelmed when she and her family had only two weeks to find a place to live while their home was remediated—a rigorous process that would take nine months. After years of being highly skilled at controlling every aspect of her life, her home, and her job, Margo could not control the mounting factors contributing to her failing health. The telling truth swept over her like a tsunami. Whatever this thing was that was happening to her life, it was bigger than she was.

The day she bottomed out, Margo lay down on her bed and really talked to God for the first time. Her plea was a desperate act of surrender, of finally letting go. As she reached out, Margo made a deal with God: First, if he would show her the clues that would lead her to get her life on path, she would listen and follow those clues. Second, if her health was restored, she would never again return to living her old way of life.

Later, Margo realized that it was in that moment that the true healing began. She received the message saying that after all she endured, God wanted to show her a different, better, healthier way to live.

Margo left the world of television and over time reinvented her life, step by step, all the while following the clues that were presented to her. Her new life was to be more about God's plan and less about achievement. She found herself slowing down, taking the time to become aware of the messages around her, and finding a sweeter way of giving her gifts to the world. There was to be more openness, more compassion, and more kindness in this new way of living. A part of her identity attached to her professional accomplishments would be lost, but that did not mean Margo would be lost. In fact, Margo was closer than ever before to discovering the real, authentic self she had long left behind.

Ultimately, it took three years on the diet to balance the yeast levels in her body and to detoxify from the candida and the adrenaline she had lived on. It would still be another seven years before she fully regained her energy.

During that time, inspired by the shamanic healer in northern Arizona, Margo sought to heal not only her body, but her mind, heart, and spirit as well. Gradually, Margo shifted from pursuing her early life goal of exhibiting extraordinary performance to a new goal of cultivating the qualities of patience, resilience, and grace. The high-speed exhilaration of life in television gave way to a time of learning to listen to her body daily and easing gently back into life. After years of constant travel, Margo put down roots at home so she could support those she loved. Margo was able to give Rachel the gift of a present mother throughout her high school years. Later she was able to call upon these newfound qualities as she cared for her husband, who was diagnosed with a debilitating disease.

One of the best gifts Margo received from her experience was a willingness to embrace rest and integrate rest into her life whenever her body called for it. Her life had become unsustainable and stayed that way until she shifted her perspective on the need to rest—until she could see it not as a sign of weakness, but as integral to her healing. Once she reframed her view of rest, she discovered, with pleasant surprise, that she was finally able to align her mind with her body simply by honoring what her body needed, without resistance. Her racing brain quieted and no longer prevented her from giving over freely to resting. In time, resting evolved from an absolute necessity to a willing act of release and nurturance. Now rest for her has an intrinsic value that will sustain her forever.

The ability to give others nonjudgmental permission to rest was another valuable lesson Margo gleaned from her experience. Both her mother and her husband have been beneficiaries of Margo's ability to understand the benefits of guilt-free rest as they face the limitations that have come with aging and a progressive disease, respectively. Best of all, with regular rest, the childhood joys that had filled Margo with wonder once again emerged. She found the energy to bring dance and music back into her life, which in turn brought back that exuberant feeling of truly being alive.

Today, the voice of the shamanic healer from that fated day in the heat of her crisis still echoes in her ears: "Everything in life is about energy—energy to live life fully. When you take time to connect your mind with your body and your spirit, you respond willingly and create quiet space for the rest that you need to restore your energetic reservoir."

In Margo's case, she regained her connection to her spirit when she surrendered to a higher power and then gave herself the precious gift of healing rest. Healthy now and reinvigorated, her mission is to keep her promises to God, to continue to foster harmony within, and to be open to giving and receiving the richness of life. In doing so, she says, she lives "in a space of gratitude and grace."

Prayer for Rest

Lord, help me dwell in the space between the lines,
so I may dream my life awake with an open eye.
Let me hear your whisper when we are apart
as a gentle melody deep inside my heart.
Lord, let me linger in the place of the unknown,
so I may know the stillness
and the sense of my true home.
Drape your cloak about me like a shelter in the storm,
so I may see the safety that has been here all along.
Lord, lead me to the silence in the cradle of your arms.
While I lay my head upon your sacred heart,
may I embrace the sound of your sweet caress
and the secret wonder of the kiss of rest.

Idea for Rest: Divine Impulse

To experience the naturally flowing rhythm of life, find a quiet place where there is fresh air and flowers. Sit where you are surrounded by nature, and notice the divine impulse that fuels the expression of the natural world.

Can you spot a bee going about pollinating? Do you hear the notes of a birdsong ringing sweetly? What different phases of openness can you find in the flowers?

There may be buds held tight, awaiting a touch of sunlight before opening. Those flowers that stand tall in the peak of beauty may emit a fragrance. Pay attention to the scent in the air. Look to see if there are some fallen petals that linger after a bloom has gone full cycle. If you watch closely enough, you can almost see a garden breathe.

Can you feel the divine intricate impulse that guides nature? Does the connection between the insect world, plant life, wildlife, and the cosmic energy of forces beyond the senses become apparent as you watch the scene unfold? Ponder how you would describe to a friend what you see and feel in this moment.

Use nature as a role model for tapping into your own effortlessly evolving life rhythm, your own divine impulse. Make a plan to return to this place on another day and repeat the experience, to take note of what has changed in the scenery, as well as inside yourself, since your previous visit.

CHAPTER FOURTEEN

It's Your Turn Now: Midlife Comes Calling

You could say it is the feeling of healing, coming home to myself after a long and bitter separation, and finding a table set with linens, candlelight and lilacs just for me.

Tama J. Kieves, This Time I Dance!

You can push yourself through a call to rest during some of the younger passages in life, but not during midlife. A cry at earlier ages can be muffled beneath the business of life. To stifle it at forty or fifty only causes a fever that festers and burns from the inside out. This yearning cannot be disguised like a pimple that shows up on date night. A little dab of Clearasil and concealer will not disguise the core of a being crying out. This is a boil that will spoil your existence. The only sure way out of this anguish is living through it.

It may feel as if a new limb is growing, and you are not quite sure on what part of the body this new limb will fit. All you sense is a compelling ache that starts in the abdomen; the seat of power is looking for a place to push through into the outside world.

Relationship, career, household duties, raising children and family are all important facets of life. But work they are! There is a price you pay for years of telling the desires of your soul to hush. The mantra of every woman in midlife should be, "It's my turn now." This mantra stands regardless of your accomplishments, your failings, your contributions, or your finances. The mere arrival at this juncture in life screams, "This is your turn!"

You must begin a slow surrender. Your spirit is longing to lie still in the bosom of the universe. The answers will not come to the surface without reflection. You need time and space to rest and reflect. You need to return to the womb from which all things come and cradle your core being with tenderness. After all, it is best to go quietly into the night and rest if you wish to emerge smiling in the sun. Ruminate and celebrate as you envision what you want life to look like going forward. Share your vision with a partner or friend. Then give yourself permission to make any wardrobe changes—literal or metaphorical—that will support your quest to bring your vision to life.

Exercise: Closet Quest

First, go through your closet with an eye for which clothes represent where and who you have been. When you are at midlife, enough years have passed for you to be able ponder your life passage thus far. What brought you here to this pinnacle, this peak from which you now view your life?

Then give some thought to your most recent clothing purchases. Do these items speak to who you want to become? What does your closet say about where you are in life and how you want your future to unfold?

Look closely, and you may notice a disparity between who you have been and who you are becoming. How do you reconcile that disparity? What parts of your wardrobe do you keep? What can be tossed away? What have you outgrown but still cherish? What do you need to put to final rest with a eulogy and a funeral pyre?

As the caterpillar sheds its skin to evolve, you can let go of your coverings and embrace the new version of yourself.

CHAPTER FIFTEEN
Longing

The best way to strengthen intuitive power is just to sit still and listen. Turn within and pay attention.
Susan Smith Jones, PhD, *The Joy Factor*

There is a place called Sedona, in northern Arizona, that is considered by many to be sacred land. My interest in Sedona began when I was reading an early publication written by Dick Sutphen. He and his wife, Tara, discovered Sedona to be a location that supported their spiritual work, and they often conducted workshops in the area. The support they received came through a palpable vibration generated by the spectacular rock formations. Native Americans have long known of the power of Sedona. There they conducted sacred ceremonies and lived lifetimes connected to the nature spirits of the earth.

I long to be in Sedona when my energy is depleted and my heart is crying out for self-love. My longing indicates that my energy is in need of restoration. I close my eyes and see the red rocks glistening in the sun and long for the nature gods of that area to nurture my spirit.

There is a clear distinction between the joyous emerging of desire and the desperate feeling of longing. Desire is born of creative impulse. Longing indicates a perceived lack. This lack may appear to be the result of someone missing in your life or the geographical separation between you and your ideal home. In truth, all lack and longing is the unfulfilled need to connect with our spirit. Only your spiritual connection with all that is can stop the longing in your heart. This direct experience of spirit can best be characterized as pure love.

The sense of oneness with all that is permeates your being in Sedona. During one memorable visit, my husband and I chose to hire a guide to hike with us through Oak Creek Canyon. With the creek itself running alongside us, we stepped upon the rocky path. The guide received intuitive messages for us as we traveled. He called this experience a walking, channeled meditation. As the trickling of the water soothed us, we opened up to hear what proved to be perfect advice for that particular life passage. When I long for Sedona, I know I am longing for direction and to be reenergized.

Another place I long for in my dreams is my grandmother's country house in upstate New York. Many frivolous and joyous times of my life were spent in that humble one room house overlooking Lake Carmel. Days were spent making mud pies, exploring, swimming, and swinging in the hammock. There I embraced a lust for life like no other. In the evenings, my sister Linda and I would lay huddled in a twin bed as sleep crept over us. There was a picture on the wall above the bed that both of us would stare at as our eyelids drooped. It showed a rudimentary sailboat traversing a small lake. Stillness was painted over the water like a protective cover. One could easily imagine the serenity of that soft sailing. There were tufts of pine trees in the background. I remember feeling the healing energy of the trees just by looking at them in the picture frame.

The feeling I had inside when I studied that picture was one of safety and contentment. When I am longing for my grandmother's house on the hill, my true longing is for a restful heart.

Exercise: The Need Within the Longing

When you are feeling low, what or where do you long for? What unfulfilled need lies beneath that longing? What is hiding there? How can you heed the message of your inner yearning?

Idea for Rest: Enjoy the View

Find a quiet place to look out upon natural beauty. You can be seated in a bench atop a rolling hill, lingering beside a forest trail, or resting at the foot of a jetty as the waves thunder to shore. Wherever it is, drink in the palette around you. Color is candy for the eyes. Indulge your sweet tooth with the majesty before you. Allow the view to captivate you. Surrender to this moment and savor it. Enjoy!

Chapter Sixteen
Prescription for Play

*If in fact the highest, most creative work is the work
of consciousness, then slowing down we're not doing
less, we're doing more. Having slowed down physically,
we're in a better space to rev up psychically.*

Marianne Williamson, *The Age of Miracles*

The American work ethic started out as a positive movement, but has become distorted over time. The push to work more and mass-produce ushered in the industrial age and made our country a mammoth empire. But the work ethic that brought us here will not take us where we want to go from here. Hanging on to our outmoded way of operating is like using obsolete technology, counterproductive to the point of becoming destructive. It seems to me that some of the most difficult, deep, important, and life-altering work we do now is done when we look like we aren't doing anything. Perhaps we are in need of a new work ethic, one that includes rest and also includes play.

Up to this point, our discussion of rest has centered on curtailing unhealthy activity patterns and giving ourselves time for rejuvenation and renewal. Simply recovering from activity overload and refueling for the next round of energy depletion is like treating the symptom instead of the disease. The key to sustaining vibrant energy is a long-term lifestyle that balances activity with rest.

For many of us, stopping our lives, halting the madness of constant motion, and being present to our own needs is a significant first step in creating the balance we crave. The next step is going beyond "not doing" to connecting with that inner child who loves to play. Playfulness allows us to slip outside the confines of our everyday responsibilities and dip into a well of creative energy to support our long-term health and wellbeing. Allowing ourselves to play does what no other form of rest can do. We give ourselves permission to embark on an unencumbered exploration of our innermost desires, those that lay buried beneath the business of life, in the land where joy resides.

For those who have sedentary jobs or who regularly spend much of their day in silence, resting through meditation or in stillness may not provide the balance that is necessary to feed the unmet needs of the spirit. Making time to twiddle or engage in frivolity may prove far more restful and effective for rejuvenation. If you are caught up in the "work hard, play hard" mentality and think that unless you are playing with a purpose (like getting fit or improving your skills at a given hobby) you're wasting your time, remembering how to play like a child is for you.

Five-Day Prescription for Play

1. Meander: To wander; to wind and turn in a course.
2. Twiddle: To gently twirl and play with something idly.
3. Daydream and Stargaze: To play with the imagination while awake.
4. Watch the Wind: To look attentively and wait expectantly to notice the movement of air.
5. Engage in Frivolity: To indulge in silliness; to lack seriousness or sense.

The following chapters explore each step in this prescription in more detail. As you approach the prescription for play, decide how much time you want to allocate to each activity listed. Use the following guidelines: an hour minimum, a day maximum. For some practices, such as the "Meander" activity, a half-day is optimum. Should one activity per day prove overwhelming, try doing one activity per week. The key is to allow time to integrate any discoveries you make along the way.

The ideal week allows time for activity, play, and rest. When you complete your five days of play, as prescribed, you can move on to the rest practices described in the two chapters that follow, "Sit in Silence" and "Intimacy with the Unknown." These chapters are designed to give you two days of reflecting and going within to further integrate what you have discovered during the play period that precedes them.

Get used to giving yourself permission to play and permission to do nothing. Let go of believing you have to fill up every spare moment of your time with activity tied to results. There is a difference between passively doing nothing and actively doing nothing. Learn to say to yourself, "I am purposefully doing nothing" or "I'm doing nothing and doing it purposely!" Set your intention to play or to rest, knowing that all is well.

Chapter Seventeen
Meander

If we know exactly where we're going, exactly how to get there, and exactly what we'll see along the way, we won't learn anything.

M. Scott Peck

An old dictionary I found defines *meandering* as "wandering and winding in a course." We can make our meandering meaningful by allowing ourselves open time without an agenda.

Have you ever found yourself choosing to take the long way home? It's late, you have put in a good day's work, and you want to unwind by driving a bit longer. You are presented with the perfect opportunity to say to yourself in a gentle voice, "Now is time to take the long way home." In taking the long way around, you allow yourself both time and freedom to experience the drive home from a different vantage point. By going beyond the same routine, you step outside the structure of your life and into the space where life transforms.

According to Esther and Jerry Hicks, in their bestselling book *Ask and It Is Given*, "Often you are in your highest state of connection to source energy while you are driving your vehicle." By *source energy*, they mean the vibrant power we all possess to manifest anything and everything in our lives. It is literally our life force. The Hicks book tells us that the rhythm of the road and the idea of going someplace new can cause you to leave behind thoughts of things that have been bothering you.

To allow time for driving without an agenda is to allow time for being without thought. Fully focusing the conscious mind on the physical task of driving frees up the subconscious, creative mind to meander, which very well may lead to unanticipated discovery. A light bulb in the brain can show up at any turn. You will recognize such a light when you say "Aha! That is the answer I was waiting for!" The discovery may not appear as your car rumbles along the back roads, but do not feel daunted. It may be hours or even days later that the time you spent driving without a specific purpose or destination will bear a gift. The trick is not to seek the discovery, the gift, as you're driving, but just accept the sheer delightful freedom of the open road and open mind. Just know that you are creating the opening for gifts to appear.

Sunday afternoons were made for meandering. When I imagine meandering, the picture I see is an open meadow framed by a forest. There are butterflies landing on newly opened flower buds. A soft breeze moves through the wild grasses. The scene beckons me to stroll and offers the chance to watch the world of nature sprites.

For others, meandering can mean window-shopping and treasure hunting in malls or shopping areas. Shopping has become an American sport, and those who excel know the best buys are found when you are not looking for them. This, too, is the magic of meandering.

Whether we are meandering down the road in our car, along the trails of a nature park, or in and out of stores lining a city street, we are allowing our experience to unfold without effort—and that is the key to and the beauty of meandering.

Although meandering is primarily a form of mental rest that frees the mind from overthinking everyday living, the playfulness of meandering restores the spirit as well. For those who have highly physical occupations or frequently engage in high-impact activity, slowing down the pace is an opportunity to dial down the body's energy output, which provides an element of physical rest. As an added bonus, the spirit is positioned to receive insight and inspiration along the way.

Idea for Rest: Meander

Did you ever notice that the word *meander* begins with the word *me*? *Meander* means "me time."

Choose a desirable destination; it may be in an outdoor garden, the halls of a cathedral, or the hallways of a nearby mall. The where does not matter—only the how is meaningful. Dedicate a specific period of time to meandering there. When you arrive, say to yourself, "While I'm here, I will move at my own pace. This time is for wandering without worry. I will allow my feet to take me where they will. I may weave this way or that, all the while knowing I am free to come or go. I will roam and ramble about, freely enjoying a rhythm all my own."

Gifts of the Garden

Take my hand.
Let me walk beside you in the garden.
Soothe your soul with the essence of light
emanating from all the glories that surround us.
Here in the garden
you are nurtured by the loving womb of creation.
Feed on the gentle scent that floats in the breeze.
Taste of the spices now seeding the earth.
Go and dance among the rose petals,
in the bliss that sifts through the treetops.
For here in the garden
the fruit of abundance is borne anew every day.
Take my hand.
Let me walk beside you in the garden.
All dreams are blossoming
to give selflessly to those who linger
in gratitude.

CHAPTER EIGHTEEN
Twiddle

So you see the imagination needs moodling—long, inefficient, happy idling, dawdling and puttering.

Brenda Ueland, *If You Want to Write*

There is an old favorite movie of mine from 1989 called *Uncle Buck*, starring John Candy as the movie's hero. Uncle Buck is given the task of watching over his brother's three children while their parents are away. The scene that stands out in my mind begins with Buck sitting in the waiting room of the elementary school principal. The meeting has been called to address the behavior of his six-year-old niece. The principal is a rigid woman wearing a high-neck collar and her hair in a tight bun. She peers at Buck over her spectacles and says in a stern voice, "Your niece is a twiddler, a dreamer, a silly heart, and a jabber box. I don't think she takes a thing in her life or her career as a student seriously."

Buck is incredulous and replies, "She's only six!" Then he says, "I don't want to know a six-year-old who isn't a twiddler or a silly heart." He tells her he knows a good kid when he sees one, because, as he puts it, "They are all good kids until some dried out, brain-dead hag . . . drags them down and convinces them they're no good." You can't help but cheer as the camera follows Buck stomping down the hallway in victory.

Yes, most of us would agree there is value in allowing our children to play. Yet we adults need time to twiddle just much as kids do. We need to twiddle just as much—or maybe more—at age thirty-six or sixty-six as we did at age six.

Why must we make life so serious? Give yourself some time to twiddle, play idly, and be a silly heart. I love to putter about my home in Houston without an agenda. I enjoy going from one room to the next, admiring the color of paint I chose for the walls or rearranging the displays of my favorite treasures. Perhaps you prefer to fiddle with a flower arrangement, dabble with a drawing, or meddle in the junk drawer next to the kitchen sink.

What comes to mind for you? What is your playful way to rest and relax? Is there a new hobby you might want to try your hand at? Now is the time to give yourself permission to do so.

Twiddling evokes the image of doing nothing but twirling, toying, or rotating our thumbs. Yet this simple liberation from the everyday pressures is exactly what we need to rejuvenate ourselves. Twiddling is about going a step beyond just chilling out and actively rekindling your creative inspiration. It is a journey into the wellspring of your being.

The Merry Butterfly Heart

The butterfly bush is ensconced with crimson flowers.
As the tiny creature draws near to it,
a dance begins.
Her wings open and close in flirtation—
feathers on the breeze
"Shall I taste this one or that?" she muses.
Gaze in her direction.
Allow your sight to rest on her graceful movement,
as the silent observer of her joyful play.
In this way, you will know
the merry heart of the butterfly.

CHAPTER NINETEEN
Daydream and Stargaze

As if through a kaleidoscope, I watched as fractaling stars spread into rays of color. A vision began to spin a circle, unfolding the Great Mystery.

Rod Bearcloud Berry, 7 *Fires*

Who among us has not suddenly found ourselves staring blankly off into the distance? It may have begun as a glance out the window between phone calls, then a mysterious force seduced us into the nothingness for an immeasurable length of time. Into the open, unlimited space went our thoughts.

The blank stare is the precursor to the daydream. Daydreaming is a magical exercise that allows our imagination the freedom to have its way with us. In order for

Permission to Rest

us to daydream, there must be dallying space between our thoughts.

The next time you catch yourself in one of these brief daydreaming interludes, make note of the thoughts and pictures that surface in your mind. Perhaps you would be served by exploring such notions further at another time.

Webster defines *stargazing* as "daydreaming; the act of looking off into the distance at the stars." When was the last time you watched the night sky? You may want to make a date with the moon, if only to marvel at her. You may want to connect with a primal need to spend time in the wonder of the stars. The ancient ones used the movement of the planets to determine when to plant their crops. The movements of the stars were closely watched and revered by our wise ancestors. Gazing at the night sky—what a wonderful way to rest your weary mind.

When I went out to the native lands of Arizona, I went on a stargazing tour. A small group of us huddled in the quiet dark of the desert canyon. We viewed Jupiter, surrounded by her four Galilean moons, orbiting close to the earth. For the first time, I saw a globular star cluster and planetary nebula. Who knew such exotic forms existed in our skies? With advanced telescopic equipment, we were treated to a view of majestic proportions. A special glass called a spectrum allowed us a glimpse of starlight that shot forth in all the colors of the rainbow. The experience left me in awe.

How many gifts of beauty have we overlooked because we are caught up in our busy lives? There is wisdom right outside our doors, waiting to be unlocked in those moments that we connect with the world beyond our everyday cares.

Idea for Rest: Stargazing

Tonight before going to sleep, sneak outside. Stare up into the open, unlimited space above you. Stare off into the distance of the night sky. Choose a star and fix your gaze upon it with eyes open wide. Allow your imagination the freedom to have its way with you. In the expanse of the mysterious Milky Way, allow yourself to dream. It will be a daydream in the dark of the night. Who has been here before you? Who will come after you have gone? With the innocence of a child, allow yourself to wonder in awe at your world.

Chapter Twenty
Engage in Frivolity

Your entire life is a work of art. And as is true of all masterpieces, everything has meaning and is important, which includes your me-time, shopping, day dreaming, dessert selections, idle chats and walkabouts.

Mike Dooley, "Notes from the Universe," TUT (tut.com)

In a world that measures worth by asking the question, "What have you produced?" we are led to label certain activity, or lack thereof, as frivolous. As a young woman embarking on a business career, I often viewed worth through the lenses of dollar signs. If there was no money to show for the action, it was a waste of time.

The first shift of my perspective on the frivolous concerned the concept of beauty. Nature created beauty, artists created beauty, and beauty came forth from a rich imagination. Yet I could not grasp the value of time spent in the presence of beauty. I thought such activity was pure indulgent frivolity. Only serious work that produced measurable results, preferably in the form of financial profit, was worthwhile. Indulging in beauty fell into the category of entertainment, mindless moments of idleness that could best be put to better use.

A decade later, I made a new friend who epitomized and appreciated beauty in a way that stunned me. Her captivating eyes and graceful features caught the gaze of every passerby. This woman took great pains to enhance her attributes with impeccable grooming and fashion sense. She was a joy to behold, but her beauty only began on the surface. She was gifted with the ability to notice the beauty in everything that she encountered. She could look at a flower or a rock, a piece of cut glass or a gemstone, and see the beauty in it. And she shared her observations with all of those around her. Her vision was an inspiration. I watched her time and time again lift the spirits of those around her with her natural focus on the quality of beauty.

Not long after meeting my friend, I began to see beauty through different lenses. Beauty had the power to transform. I could walk into a garden and, upon seeing a flurry of flowers, become delighted. The act of walking into the door of a beautiful room could bring a rush of vitality. Color, texture, and object placement had a profound impact on the quality of the space and the activity within. With these realizations, a whole new world opened up to me.

This awakening came to mind when I began to recreate my thoughts around the idea of rest. The world I lived in viewed rest as a waste of time. Rest was flat out frivolous. When I would feel the need to slow down, I would simultaneously hear the admonishment, "Shouldn't you be doing something productive?" It seemed that whatever I was doing was more important than resting. "For God sakes," I would think to myself, "don't stop now, or you will never get it done!"

On the surface, to be frivolous seems to entail abandoning all discipline. But it actually takes great discipline for most of us to allow ourselves those qualities we falsely believe are luxuries meant for the rich and famous. The truth is, rest is not a luxury. Rest is a biological, emotional, and spiritual need.

For me, learning to value rest began with the support of a therapist I sought out to help me cope with my stress level. From our sessions emerged the idea to cut back my workweek to four days, giving me a three-day weekend during which to regenerate. My first objection was financial: wouldn't less work mean less pay? This wise counselor convinced me to experiment with the concept. Imagine my surprise when I discovered I was, in fact, surrounded by a world of examples of people who worked less than I did yet had more financially rewarding lives. A day off, a day to rest, did not automatically equate to financial disaster. Furthermore, someone with a four-day workweek was not necessarily thought of as a slacker.

Thus began my journey into allowing frivolity into my life—first with beauty, then with rest, and finally with laughter. Stories were emerging in the alternative-health circles about laughter as a tool for healing. Turns out, the endorphins released during a belly laugh contain the power to transform the cells of the body. You can literally laugh yourself back to health!

Exercise: What Frivolity Can Be

What is your definition of frivolous? Is it possible that being frivolous could contribute to your wellbeing? Make a list of things you can do for the pure joy of the activity or perhaps simply to give yourself a good laugh. Do one thing on your list, and notice how you feel afterward. Make notes about the effect it has on your day or your week. Is being frivolous a waste of time or a window into a world you want to explore more?

Idea for Rest: Sit in a Swing

When was the last time you sat on a swing? For most of us, it has been far too long. The swing was one of my favorite childhood playground toys. Early memories conjure up images of neighborhood parks and schoolyards on windy days. It seemed soaring on that seat was the closest I could get to flying.

Later in life, I learned there was something about swaying that would soothe my thoughts regardless of what matter I was mulling over. It was not uncommon for me to drive to the nearest shoreline, sit upon a swing, and match the sweeping of my motion to the rhythm of the waves rolling in. Swinging with the smell of salt in the air and the breath of the breeze on my face was pure joy.

Find a swing or a place where you can rock or sway as you sit. Settle yourself into the sweetness this gentle movement brings. Later, reflect on your experience. What physical sensations did you feel? Did memories come to mind? How did you feel emotionally while swinging? How did this activity affect your ability to sense your spirit?

CHAPTER TWENTY-ONE

Watch the Wind

*Wind moving through the grass
so that the grass quivers . . .
moves me with an emotion I
don't ever understand.*

From the journal of Katherine Mansfield, 1922

Nature is a gateway to the spirit. Observing nature may well be the easiest, yet most powerful way of leading ourselves within.

The soft red feathers of the robin's breast remind us that nature is gentle. The breeze blows loose twigs and leaves out of the trees. When the robin is gathering twigs in my yard, I know spring is around the corner. The wind will carry seeds as it flutters between the leaves and branches that hover over my back yard. The robin seems to sense when the seeds have made their home in the earth and are nudging against its crust, waiting and willing to give life.

It is the wind that gives the robin the inspiration to fly freely with a worm in her beak. Watching this process, I am in awe of the connection between the wind, the earth, the birds, and the seeds of life. I am witness to a truly masterful creation in action.

Though we cannot see the wind in the way we see our fine feathered friends, we feel it much more deeply. The wind is an invisible yet powerful force that will determine the direction of both the life of the plant and that of these fabulous flying creatures. The wind has a mind of its own and survival often depends on our willingness to accept the direction it offers. To resist the will of the wind results in struggle for all of nature, including the human beings privileged to share this planet.

How can it be that a force invisible to the naked eye so strongly impacts the world? You will learn this firsthand by watching the wind. Since you truly cannot see something that is invisible, often you must look for subtle movements in your environment to detect its presence. For example, you must finely tune your sense of touch so you will feel the gentleness of the breezes as they pass. Watching the wind is an art form that teaches you to appreciate the invisible powers of the essence of life around you. When you have watched for a while, you can almost feel the wind hold you in the palm of its hand. Now that is a magical moment.

Idea for Rest: Time in Nature

Allow yourself to walk in nature. Carve out some time and have no agenda. Go somewhere low key and with plenty of space to wander, such as an arboretum, garden, wooded area, or park. When you get there, listen. Notice the sounds you hear in the air. Notice the sounds coming from within yourself.

If you keep a journal, write about the sounds after your walk. I created this poem upon returning from a nature walk. Perhaps you too will be so inspired.

Heart Whisper

I hear a voice
whispering on the edge of the breeze
That lingers in my backyard.
"Come this way" is the call
to step into
the soft footprints
going this way and that,
winding ahead,
across the horizon,
to a place unknown.
"Trust in me,"
it breathes lovingly.
Gentleness reaches out to me,
and tugs at my heart.

CHAPTER TWENTY-TWO

Sit in Silence

Here's a paradox of this path: doing nothing does something. When I say doing nothing, I don't mean kicking back and watching Entertainment Tonight or reading Tom Clancy novels. Let's be clear here. When I say, "doing nothing," I mean cultivating silence and space.

Tama J. Kieves, *This Time I Dance!*

One morning I woke to the distinctive sound of a drill bit boring into the earth. As I opened my eyes to seek the source of the construction noise, I saw a large raven carrying a piece of rope in her mouth.

"The ravens are building a new nest," I said to my husband. "Look." I pointed through the window to the top of a large pine tree that borders our back property line.

Our home is located in a tiny village within ten miles of the fourth-largest city in the United States. The village was established over fifty years ago when the location was considered "out in the country." Today the area is covered in tall trees and comprises streets that wind between charming homes, and property in the area is highly coveted for its proximity to the city. We are undergoing what many cities in this country have experienced. Here in Houston, they call it "tear downs." A tear down is the removal of a quaint old home in order to build a multi-million-dollar monstrosity in its place. Perhaps one man's castle is nothing but a cave to another. My friends tell me I should be glad the neighborhood is appreciating in value. Yet all I see is the disappearance of open space and wildlife habitat.

I am grateful the builders of the new home behind ours left a few of the original trees on the lot they leveled for construction. One of those trees had the home of the ravens high in its branches. The birds were as upset as I was when the machines blared through the morning air. It was clear they could not live that close to the commotion.

If birds are offended by obtrusive sounds, what of us humans? We, too, must build our nest in a quieter place. If this is not possible, we must carve out a silent place to go and be quiet.

Idea for Rest: Let the Rocks Restore You

After you've taken time to watch the fluid energy of the wind and witness the changes it brings to the environment, take time to notice the complimentary force of stillness by spending time with the stable, ancient energy of rocks. Promise yourself fifteen minutes alone near a rock.

If you have a rock yard in your area, go there and browse until you find a rock that speaks to you. Or you may prefer to visit the rocks of cliffs along a beach or those on an urban playground. All that you need is the willingness to take a gentle stroll. Choose a place to sit and listen.

A stone is the epitome of serenity. Give the rock your full attention and note any message it chooses to impart. A message may come in one of many forms, from a random thought to a feeling in your physical body. Wait patiently for it, as a rock waits for eternity.

Silence

When a sight or a sound
pulses through my being
like a shooting star,
it is then that I know the bounty,
and it claims me
to be a flower blossoming
in the Garden of Eden.

CHAPTER TWENTY-THREE
Intimacy with the Unknown

The real world shows a world seen differently, through quiet eyes and with a mind at peace. Nothing but rest is there.

A Course in Miracles

There is certain trepidation when we visualize the unknown. It conjures images of darkness and abandonment. The unknown may challenge us to overcome fear. Fear of the unknown is, in fact, unfounded, for to be in the place of the unknown is to be the closest to safety we ever experience.

The womb of life itself is such a place. Our mother's womb is the first place we receive nurturing in the form of love from our parents—despite the fact that they do not yet know us. It is the first place we receive the nourishment necessary to support physical life. Yet it is also one of the darkest and most mysterious places that exist.

We learn intimacy in the womb. Our spirit connects with human life. This is a unique and profound connection.

When we enter the state of silent rest, we approach this place of the safe yet mysterious unknown once more. It is here in the stillness that we develop our intimacy with our own essence and that of the universe. It is here that we have the chance to adhere closely to our innermost being, to dive deep into our private spiritual source. We then quietly nurture a sense of trust and strengthen our willingness to first face our fears and then embrace our gifts. Our intuition will blossom here in this sacred space.

To create your own state of womblike rest, set the intention to be with yourself quietly in loving kindness, as a mother would be with her unborn child. A developing child in the womb grows familiar with the rhythm and sway of her mother's hips as she walks. You may want to recreate the feeling of being cradled and rocked in much the same way. Or perhaps you can pretend you are a caterpillar that has just spun a warm, safe cocoon in which to rest and transform.

Choose a comfortable space to lie down or sit in an overstuffed rocking chair. Make certain you are in a place where you know you are not going to be startled or interrupted. The area should be as soundless and impenetrable as possible. Wrap yourself in a soft, swaddling blanket. Be sure you are snug and warm. The ideal atmosphere is one of total safety. To calm your mind, you can listen to a recording of a human heartbeat or the rhythm of the waves coming ashore at the ocean. However you set the stage, time spent in the unknown is the ultimate in physical inactivity.

When you enter the realm of the unknown, you may see brilliant colors. Often I find myself tingling at the top of my head or in other unrelated body parts. On occasion, I hear the soft murmur of energy pulsing around me. Sometimes a blissful feeling washes over my being, and I become a witness to the awesome beauty, power, and magnificence of the universe.

In time, you may want to linger in the unknown long enough to know you can learn to trust the forces that created you and learn to connect with the love that resides there. In the silence you will hear more than you ever imagined. Hone your sense of listening in this dimension, for it is a gift that will lead you to the secrets of yourself.

Idea for Rest: Sequester Yourself

Today, set yourself apart from your day-to-day life. Today, sequester yourself in a sacred space. Know that you deserve this time to be still and to listen to the quiet majesty of eternity. You deserve to take time to soar freely in the infinite, where you can rediscover the light you truly are.

You may be called to choose a poem, a piece of scripture, or a passage from a favorite inspiring book, and hold it close to your heart, sharing yourself with the symmetry of the words as they touch you. You deserve this seclusion in the sanctuary of your spirit. Become the observer of your experience. Stay there as long as you like or as long as time will permit.

Here We Are

So this is how we are
falling softly into each other's arms
after yet another lifetime
of dreaming memories
it has come to this
for you and me
as stillness falls
like a tender mist
in our hearts
we have a history
the story of us
midway on our journey
to the stars
questions left dangling
unattached
a sense of knowing
answers don't matter anymore
and here we are
listening to the rain
falling gently into the unknown
and never being more certain
of everything
and of nothing
as we are now.

CHAPTER TWENTY-FOUR

Will the Real Me Please Stand Up?

Though the human body is born and complete in the moment, the birth of the human heart is an ongoing process.

John O'Donohue, *Anam Cara, A Book of Celtic Wisdom*

Rest and play both give us a glimpse into our true selves. One wise man said the degree to which you question yourself determines who you will become. Asking the tough, bold questions is an act of courage.

Who am I? This question beckons us first in adolescence and comes back to us at every life transition. If we have been speeding through our midlife with the proverbial pedal to the metal, it tends to rear its ugly head at the first stop sign.

To answer this question for myself, I took the challenge writer Mary Pipher poses in her book *Writing to Change the World*. Mary asks her readers to embark on a voyage of discovery, beginning with revisiting their childhood roots in the chapter entitled "Know Thyself." The following poem came from my heart in response.

Who Am I?

I am from the North and the South,
> from the youth and the skyscrapers of New York City,
> from the sandy beaches of the island that rests nearby.

I am from adventure. My grandparents traveled the waters of the world to land at the Statue of Liberty.

I am from Italy and Scotland, for their blood runs through my veins. And so does Native American blood somewhere back there in South Carolina.

I am from sexy jokes that make you laugh until your sides hurt, from card games and betting on the horses.

I am from lighting a candle in front of the Madonna at mass.

Will the Real Me Please Stand Up?

I am from mysteries that were held in silent
    prayer—with a glass of wine—on Sunday.
I am from trees and flowers and the little creatures
    that roam the earth beneath my feet,
    from riding my bike through the forest paths
    and swinging in the hammock.
I am from rock 'n' roll music, classic country
    western, and Italian Christmas songs.
I am from dancing a jig to the bagpipes in my
    grandmother's living room.
I am from inspiration and plenty of parties.
I am from *Swan Lake, Man of La Mancha,* and *Romeo and Juliet.* I am from watching the *Wizard of Oz*
    over and over again.
I am from running the halls at the Museum of
    Natural History, riding waves in the ocean,
    and swimming in the lake.
I am from counting money and eating well no
    matter what.
I am from a group of givers with most generous
    hearts.
I am from independence, from pulling oneself up
    by the bootstraps.
I am the girl who wore a suit and carried a
    briefcase in a man's world.
I am the one who knocked on doors and dealt with
    rejection.

I am from the world of magic and miracles.
I am from my love affair with the Southwest.
I am from the sultry summers of Houston, where I choose to live.
I am from the silent walks on the beach at midnight.
I am from my retreats in the red rocks of Sedona.
I am from Carlos Casteneda, Caroline Myss, Wayne Dyer, and all my New Age heroes.
I am from my brazen and often outlandish escapades.
I am from my dark nights of the soul.
I am from my many meditations on the mountaintops.
I am from my hands digging deep down into the earth and then raising my glass above to celebrate life with friends.
I am a wife, mother, grandmother, sister, and daughter of the universe.
I am from the blissful moments shared with those I love.

Try your own hand at this exercise. Reviewing your life experience from a heightened vantage point will help you garner insight and gain influence over who you become. To do the exercise justice, find a quiet place and time to devote to self-reflection.

CONCLUSION

Sunset in Sedona

So God blessed the seventh day and hallowed it, because on it God rested from all the work that he had done in creation.

Genesis 2:3

In the summer of 2006, I sat in my rose garden in Houston and sent out a prayer. I had taken an "Artist's Way" class, based on the famous 1992 book by Julia Cameron. I had formed a group of artists to meet in my home, and I had begun dabbling with writing *Permission to Rest*. The concept and essays were becoming near and dear to me, yet I knew, in my heart of hearts, I could not do the topic justice without giving myself permission to rest. The words I spoke in prayer were a request for the courage and financial support to embark on a month-long sabbatical from my financial business. This time was to be devoted to the path of writing. I knew exactly the place I wanted to be for this sojourn. My husband and I had vacationed many times in the mystical red rocks of Sedona, Arizona. During each visit there, I would find inspiration stirring. Sedona had become my heart place.

To request time and money for a month-long trip to Sedona was asking a lot from the powers that be. After all, I had a daughter enrolled in private college, clients to care for, and a house note to cover. When the global financial collapse hit in 2008, my dream was delayed. Despite these setbacks, I drew support from my dear husband, Dennis; my friends; and my writing mentors. I found myself in a position to actualize this undertaking during the autumn of 2010.

My spirit danced during those September days in the desert, delighting in the gift of rest I had received. As the magical month drew to an end, I savored the final sunsets that so often grace the homelands of ancient wisdom.

Sunsets are sacred to me in Sedona. One final night, I poured a glass of wine and watched from the front porch of the rental home as the twilight approached. The full color spectrum of the rainbow streaked across the sky. All shades from crimson to violet cut a path through the cumulous clouds. In the distance I heard the hoot of an owl and the howl of a coyote. The crickets and cicadas began their chorus. I watched the color forms change shape and shade as the final rays of the sun began to fade. I sat still, keeping watch in silence until the last of the day slipped away.

"I want to remember this view when I get back to city life," I thought to myself. "This sunset must be etched so deep in my cells that I can call it up at will."

When the night had swallowed the day whole, I wondered if the course of my life could be changed in that mere month out in Sedona. I heard the response as a whisper, murmured by the angel of truth from a far away place within.

Yes, a month out here can change the course of your life, Debra Mae. In fact, the course of your life can be changed in one moment—one exquisite moment of rest.

As you go about creating your own resting practice, may you too be transformed. For the aim of this work is an opening. The opening is created inside of you, the reader, in a place that deserves to be heard and cared for. Every journey is unique, known only to the one who chooses to travel. The meanings of signs and symbols along the way will be yours alone to discover. How your spirit will meet these experiences is a mystery to be revealed.

Perhaps when you need a hand to hold, one of my poems will hold you dear. When you need some support, maybe something said on the page will rise up to meet you. My hope is that my heart will reach out to yours and we will touch each other in tenderness. Together we will create a richer more restful life for ourselves and the world.

Acknowledgments

In the moment before the story began, I was an eight-year-old girl who loved to walk in the garden. My mother suggested I make a book for my grandfather, Vincent Pepe, who cherished reading. I wrote about morning glories and penned my first poem across the page of a rudimentary drawing of that mysterious purple flower. The seed of inspiration was planted within me that fine summer day.

First and foremost, I wholeheartedly thank and acknowledge my mother, Edna "Candi" White, for instilling in me the love of books and the desire to write.

There were occasional writing spurts over the course of my early life, but the first time I dove in was at the encouragement of my client, Susan Lowe. Susan is a published author with fourteen books in print. She suggested we form a writing group back in the early 1990s.

Susan and her friend Devoni Wardlow extended tireless counsel to me over the many years and incarnations of our writing-group gatherings. They showed patience with my spelling (before the days of spell check) and twelfth-grade-education grammar, and their coaching was a true labor of love. They were also the first two friends to edit the earliest version of my manuscript. Thank you, Susan and Devoni, for never giving up on me!

It's been almost a decade since I signed up for an *Artist's Way* class, based on the book by Julia Cameron, at Unity Church of Christianity. The group from the class continued to meet in my home for years thereafter, encouraging each other weekly in our creative pursuits. A special thank you to Shannon Modrell, Lisa Canida, Tim Johnson, Cynthia Hinesley, Betsy Volz, and Kellie Koppel for their support when the idea of *Permission to Rest* began taking form.

The day in 2009 that I met Janet Conner, author of *Writing Down Your Soul*, *The Lotus and the Lily*, and *Soul Vows*, forever changed my life. Janet told me I wasn't crazy for hearing voices in my head telling me to write. Janet's writing classes gave me the confidence and resources to realize my dream of publishing *Permission to Rest*. I owe Janet a debt of gratitude for generously sharing her time and talent and for teaching me how to access amazing spiritual guidance.

Acknowledgments

Janet Conner's classes also connected me via the Internet with kindred spirits that span the globe. Thank you to Margaret Duarte, author of the *Enter the Between* series; the first of her four novels, *Between Now and Forever,* is now in print. Margaret's work is destined to change the face of education for generations to come. Thank you to Shanee Barclough of Christchurch, New Zealand, keeper of the poetry blog *Throw Me to the Sky*. Shanee's poetry moves my heart like no other. She is the best poet I know yet to be published. Thank you to Amy Isaman, the English teacher turned quilter and novelist residing in the wilds of Nevada and keeper of the blog *Speaking of Words, Quilts, and Life*. You three kept reading my blog and posting comments to keep me going in those fragile days of wondering if I had anything worth saying.

During 2013, a small group of women gathered in my home to embark on the experiential aspect of *Permission to Rest*. These willing cohorts who read the exercises, shared their results, and provided ideas that I later sprinkled throughout the book were Kathy Sheppard, Shannon Whiting, Jacinda Wooloson, and my endearing esthetician, Marissa Espinoza. Your contributions to this work are appreciated more than you know.

The meditation practice I most use and mention is called Ascension. I am deeply grateful to my Ascension teachers, Kali and Bhagavati Ishaya and to all the

"Ascenders" for our many group get-togethers filled with loving rest throughout the past ten years.

My appreciation goes out to the women whose personal stories are shared within these pages. Their true names have been withheld to protect their privacy, but they made my words come to life.

Thank you to all of my fellow members and neighbors in the Hilshire Village Book Club. You have broadened my horizons.

Many thanks to my lifelong personal friends, cheerleaders, and early editors: Justine Ounsi, Tod Shannon Castle, Ricki Willoughby, and my dear sister, Linda Curto. My daughter, Noelle Marie Howland, deserves thanks for the initial edits of Adella's story. I am grateful to my niece, Cara Gourley Shannon, a gifted writer in her own right, who provided help with my poems.

Linda Starr is a longtime friend and life coach whom I consider my very first life mentor. Linda has been imparting wisdom to me and other entrepreneurs in Houston for decades. Some of the exercises and concepts in this book are based on what I learned in her classes over the years. She also came up with "pink dot days." Thank you, Linda, for being all you have been in my life. You introduced me to unlimited possibility!

Thanks go out to the valued professionals who have helped me maintain good health for many years: my monthly massage therapist, Wess Seago; Dr. Cyril Wolfe,

Acknowledgments

who gave me permission to not be perfect; and Dr. Mark Hendry, who is more than my chiropractor. Over the past twenty-plus years, Mark has become a friend and co-conspirator on my spiritual path.

Thank you to my daughter, Aleasha Stephens, the devoted social media diva who set up my blog, and Jennifer Robenalt, the public relations maven who helped kick start it with her creative marketing.

To all of my family, friends, clients, and colleagues who kept after me to tell them how the book was going, thank you. A special thanks to my partner in my financial-planning practice, John Gutfranski, who entered my life at just the right moment to help me free up the time to bring this book to fruition.

When it came down to the home stretch, *Permission to Rest* became a collaborative work between me and my beloved editor, Amy Rost. Amy, there would be no book without your meticulous editing, insightful feedback, and our rich conversations.

I've left the biggest thank you for last. Thank you to my husband, my heartthrob, and life partner, Dennis Stephens. You have been with me every step of the way, reading every word of my writing long before I'd dare to show it to anyone else. Our love has endured over twenty-five years of life's challenges. You are my eternal soul mate, and my gratitude to you is boundless.

Take a Moment

Let me just take a moment
and surround myself with gratitude.
Let the grace of my thanks
wash over me.

For those I love
And who love me
no matter what.

For the joy of living
here and now
in the glorious shadow
of eternity in the making.

Let me stare into the eyes
of the Creator
and see myself as blessed and divine.

For just a moment
let me bask in being grateful
for all that is.

Recommended Resources

Books

Physical: Care for Your Physical Wellbeing

Edlund, Matthew. *The Power of Rest: Why Sleep Alone Is Not Enough.* HarperOne, 2010.

Rankin, Lissa. *Mind Over Medicine: Proof that You Can Heal Yourself.* Hay House, 2013.

Richardson, Cheryl. *The Art of Extreme Self Care: Transform Your Life One Month at a Time.* Hay House, 2009.

Mental: Transform Your Thoughts and Beliefs

Hay, Louise L. *You Can Heal Your Life.* Hay House, 1984.

Katie, Byron. *A Thousand Names for Joy: Living in Harmony with the Way Things Are.* Harmony Books, 2007.

Katie, Byron. *Who Would You Be Without Your Story?* Harmony Books, 2008.

Starr, Linda. *The Genesis Formula: How to Create Anything You Want as Soon as Possible.* Star CTC, 2012.

Emotional: Heal Your Emotions

Brown, Brené. *Daring Greatly: How the Courage to be Vulnerable Transforms the Way We Live, Love, Parent and Lead.* Gotham Books, 2012.

NurrieStearns, Mary, and Rick NurrieStearns. *Yoga for Emotional Trauma: Meditations and Practices for Healing Pain and Suffering.* New Harbinger, 2013.

Ortner, Nick. *The Tapping Solution: A Revolutionary System for Stress-Free Living.* Hay House, 2013.

Spirit: Connect with Your Spirit

Conner, Janet. *Writing Down Your Soul: How to Activate and Listen to the Extraordinary Voice Within.* Conari Press, 2008.

Conner, Janet. *The Lotus and Lily: Access the Wisdom of Buddha and Jesus to Nourish Your Beautiful, Abundant Life.* Conari Press, 2012.

Roth, Ron. *The Healing Path of Prayer: A Modern Mystic's Guide to Spiritual Power.* Harmony Books, 1997.

Williamson, Marianne. *A Return to Love: Reflections on the Principles of "A Course in Miracles."* Random House, 1992.

Other Recommended Reading

Bolen, Jean Shiroda. *Crossing to Avalon: One Woman's Quest for the Sacred Feminine.* Harper SanFrancisco, 1994.

Cameron, Julia. *The Artists Way: A Spiritual Path to Higher Creativity.* Tarcher Putnam, 1992.

Drucker, Karen. *Let Go of the Shore: Stories and Songs to Set the Spirit Free* (book and music CD). DeVorss & Company, 2010.

Hanh, Thich Nhat. *Breathe, You Are Alive!: Sutra on the Full Awareness of Breathing.* Parallax Press, 2008.

Kidd, Sue Monk. *When the Heart Waits: Spiritual Direction for Life's Sacred Questions.* HarperOne, 1990.

Kieves, Tama J. *This Time I Dance!: Trusting the Journey of Creating the Work You Love, How One Harvard Lawyer Left It All to Have It All.* Tarcher Putnam, 2002.

Mountain Dreamer, Oriah. *What We Ache For: Creativity and the Unfolding of Your Soul.* HarperOne, 2005.

Whyte, David. *The House of Belonging.* Many Rivers Press, 1997.

Individuals

Janet Conner, author, teacher, and host of the online radio program *The Soul Directed Life,* janetconner.com.

Wayne W. Dyer, internationally renowned author and speaker in self-development, drwaynedyer.com.

Bhagavati and Kali Ishaya, "Ascension" meditation technique for enlightenment, ishaya.info.

Caroline Myss, international renowned author, speaker, and medical intuitive, myss.com.

Linda Starr, coach, trainer, and consultant, starrctc.com.

Dennis Stephens, Somato-Emotional Release and craniosacral therapist, dennisstephens.com.

Other

Brain Sync, meditation CDs and guided imagery meditation CDs, brainsync.com.

Daily Word print and online magazine with inspirational daily messages, dailyword.com.

"Oprah & Deepak: 21-Day Meditation Experience," guided meditations from Oprah Winfrey and Deepak Chopra on CDs and mp3s, chopracentermeditation.com.

Notes from the Universe, Mike Dooley, personalized, uplifting, daily email notes, TUT.com.

Relax Melodies, Relax Melodies Oriental, Relax Melodies Seasons. Smartphone apps with binaural beats and subtle background sounds for meditation and relaxation. From Ipnos Soft.

About the Author

Debra Mae White is a writer dedicated to helping women recognize and honor their need for rest. She is also a wife, mother, and Certified Financial Planner (CFP)® with forty years of experience in the financial-services industry. She lives in Houston, Texas, where she enjoys tending her beloved rose garden with her husband of over twenty-five years, Dennis Stephens, an alternative health care practitioner.

For more information, see her website and blog, Debra Mae White: Permission to Rest www.debramaewhite.com, or email her at dws@debramaewhite.com.